AGING
SAFELY
in Your Home

AGING
SAFELY
in Your Home

**Yvonne Poulin and
Gordon Morrison**

Self-Counsel Press
(a division of)
International Self-Counsel Press Ltd.
USA   Canada

Self-Counsel Press acknowledges the financial support of the Government of Canada through the Canada Book Fund (CBF) for our publishing activities.

Printed in Canada.

First edition: 2015

Library and Archives Canada Cataloguing in Publication

Poulin, Yvonne, author
    Aging safely in your home / Yvonne Poulin and Gordon Morrison.

(Eldercare series)
Issued in print and electronic formats.
ISBN 978-1-77040-219-5 (pbk.).—ISBN 978-1-77040-992-7 (epub).—ISBN 978-1-77040-993-4 (kindle)

    1. Older people—Dwellings. 2. Dwellings—Remodeling. 3. Barrier-free design for older people. 4. Exercise for older people. I. Morrison, Gordon, 1960-, author II. Title. III. Series: Eldercare series

NA7195.A4P68 2015	720.84'6	C2014-908253-3
C2014-908254-1	C2014-908254-1	C2014-908254-1

Appendix, Checklist 2, and Checklist 8 adapted from material by the Canadian Initiative for Elder Planning Studies and used with permission.

Self-Counsel Press
(a division of)
International Self-Counsel Press Ltd.

Bellingham, WA   North Vancouver, BC
USA   Canada

Contents

Notice to Readers

Laws are constantly changing. Every effort is made to keep this publication as current as possible. However, the authors, the publisher, and the vendor of this book make no representations or warranties regarding the outcome or the use to which the information in this book is put and are not assuming any liability for any claims, losses, or damages arising out of the use of this book. The reader should not rely on the author or the publisher of this book for any professional advice. Please be sure that you have the most recent edition.

Dedication

To our elderly family, friends, and clients who face the challenges of aging courageously; with dignity, grace, and a healthy dose of humor. We dedicate this book to you and to the many seniors who are proving that it is possible to age safely in their homes.

Introduction

"Aging won't happen to us; we will choose how to age."

— Unknown

We were almost finished writing this book when Gord saw an elderly woman with an enormous smile. She was using a walker and seemed to be cruising along quite comfortably. She appeared to be aging well and contentedly. I had to laugh when I focused on her T-shirt and read the printed message that seemed a testament to her vibrant outlook on life: "I got 99 problems but age ain't one of them"! At that moment Gord realized that how we age is a choice. We can't stop aging but we can always have a positive attitude about it.

Aging is a fact of life and the smiling lady brought me full circle to why we wanted to write this book. We're both aging and we'd like to do it with grace and dignity. We both wish to choose how we age. As

50-somethings, we are considered seniors in many parts of the world. In fact, it was somewhat shocking four years ago when Gord received a senior's discount at a buffet in the state of Washington! Woo-hoo!

We wish to continue our positive approach to aging and we want to inspire other seniors to take an active role in their aging process, despite the fact you may have 99 problems to deal with. Lucky for you, this is a book of solutions. These solutions can help you with aging safely in your home and maybe even put a smile on your face.

From the moment we began this book, we envisioned each chapter as a piece of a puzzle. Some aspects of the puzzle are more important than others. Having the right attitude, keeping fit, and preventing falls are enormously important. Our puzzle has a person in the middle surrounded by his or her home that keeps him or her safe and secure. Anyone who's done a puzzle knows that the joy is in the journey, not the final destination. We hope that our readers will embrace the journey of aging safely because it's an ongoing, an evolving, a dynamic, and an ever-changing adventure.

Your physical, social, emotional, mental, and spiritual reality today might not be the same tomorrow. You'll need to keep rearranging the pieces of your puzzle because you'll change as you age. Certain pieces of your aging puzzle will need more attention than others, depending on your situation at the time. This book will help you be a person who's safe and secure in your own home.

Each chapter will contribute to helping you make smart and safe choices about how you live and where you live as you age. We have provided some solutions regarding what needs to be done and how to get things done. We're hopeful that the book helps everyone find or create the right environment and home for aging safely.

You will notice that the book is written in two parts: Part 1 discusses the human aspect, and Part 2 discusses the housing aspect. The two sections recommend adaptations that will greatly enhance your ability and suitability to age safely at home. We believe these parts are interconnected to such a degree that they are needed in equal measure for aging safely in your home. The two parts will read slightly differently because they were written by different authors. *Aging Safely in Your Home* is the combined perspective of an elder-care planner and an architectural technologist.

Yvonne Poulin, as a Registered Massage Therapist and Elder Planning Counsellor, has a wide-ranging, cross-disciplinary education and experience in the human aspect. Her 25 years of clinical experience is reflected in the recommendations she makes for health and wellness, and she refers to the insights gained from her patients and clients who have demonstrated the best ways to deal with aging and disability issues. She is the director of Vancouver Dementia Care Consulting, the company through which this project originated. Yvonne has a personal history of caring for her aging parents who were eventually affected by dementia. She also shares her experience in adapting environments and mind-sets to overcome physical challenges.

Yvonne's voice will guide you through Part 1: Human Aspect of Aging Safely in Your Home — Personal Adaptations. Four broad categories will be discussed to enable you to age actively:

1. **Physical:** Be physically prepared to age safely in your home.

2. **Social:** Get support and maintain an active social network to help you age safely in your home.

3. **Emotional:** Plan to stay happily in your home.

4. **Mental and spiritual:** Keep mentally fit and nourish your spirit.

Gordon Morrison, as an architectural technologist and industrial technology educator, has a wide-ranging, cross-disciplinary education and experience in the housing aspect. He understands the value of a well thought out, well-designed, and well-built home environment. He's helped many people make home adaptations and renovations for their specific needs, and has worked on many housing improvement projects for seniors so they can age safely and thrive in their homes.

Gordon's voice will guide you through Part 2: Housing Aspect of Aging Safely in Your Home. Five broad categories will be discussed to make your home safe and suitable for you as you age:

1. **Rate your home:** Evaluate whether to stay or move.

2. **Make your home comfortable:** Create comfort and security.

3. **Adapt your home:** Make adaptations to simplify your life.

4. **Renovate your home:** Re-create your home as you age.

5. **Prevent falls:** Recognize problems and find solutions.

The two parts of this book have been written knowing that the overwhelming majority of seniors prefer to remain at home and in their familiar neighborhoods. Unfortunately, many seniors are forced to leave their homes prematurely due to falls and other factors. These unwanted situations could be either prevented or delayed through personal and home adaptations that would enable them to stay healthy and well in their current homes. The main intent of this book is to help people stay in their home as long as possible. A secondary intent is to help guide seniors, caregivers, friends, and family toward knowing when staying in the home is not the best or safest choice. Knowing when things are unmanageable is important and this book will help you assess that.

The World Health Organization defines good health as "a state of complete physical, social and mental well-being and not merely the absence of disease or infirmity."[1] Based on this definition of good health, we believe that a holistic approach is imperative. This book is more than a manual about home adaptations; it's about informing seniors of the various factors that affect their ability to age safely at home. We directly address the barriers to aging well: Physical (including the dwelling), social, mental, emotional, and spiritual isolation.

We should point out that this book has been written for seniors who are experiencing normal aging. There are many complicating factors and situations that are caused by illness or disease. They bring into the picture some special considerations that must be addressed on a case-by-case basis, preferably under the care of medical experts and care-support experts.

We are trying to point you in the right direction to get the kinds of personal and housing adaptations that will empower you to age safely in your home. This book is not a construction manual for retro-fitting your home. We do not endorse any products or services. We are simply trying to help you put the pieces of the puzzle together and help you to understand the kinds of changes that will help you as you age.

This book includes a variety of checklists, worksheets, and diagrams, which will be most useful to you if you complete the forms. (Use the download kit to print the forms and complete them by hand or by using your computer's Word program — link included at the end of this book.) Highlight parts of the book that are particularly relevant for you, or write some helpful suggestions from the book and place them on your fridge as daily reminders. Complete the Rate Yourself and Rate Your Home checklists to help you assess and monitor what adaptations need to be made in your current situation. It is wise to review these checklists on an ongoing basis because your circumstances are likely to change regularly.

---

1   World Health Organization, accessed February 2015. http://www.who.int/trade/glossary/story046/en/

If any of your answers on the rating worksheets are "no," read the corresponding information in that chapter for suggestions on how to change your answers to a "yes." You may be surprised by what a positive difference it can make to follow these recommendations.

If you, or the senior you are concerned about, are unable or unwilling to make the changes required to age safely, then it is time to move to a more suitable living situation. We've included an Appendix entitled Signs That It's Time to Move to help you determine if a senior requires professional assistance or a change in housing.

We use simple and conversational language throughout the book. There are some issues of language and terms that might need clarification. For example, a common industry term for aging safely in your home is "remaining in place" or "aging in place." Another example is our use of the word "tribe"; we refer to your tribe as your social network, related or otherwise, who help support you through your aging process. We have tried to keep our terms of reference relevant to all readers. This will not always be the case. For example, offering the suggestion to keep walkways clear of snow and sanded during the winter might not be helpful to someone living in Key West, Florida. Also, construction practices and techniques do vary from region to region so you might need to read between the lines to sort out what's relevant for your location.

No matter where you live or what stage you're at in your journey, creating the right human and housing aspects for aging safely in your home is a customized journey requiring you and/or your caregivers to do most of the work. We believe that with a positive attitude, aging safely in your home can be a pleasant and rewarding experience. We encourage you to join us as we look for T-shirts that say: "I got 99 problems but age ain't one of them." We like the image of us all wearing the right attitude for aging safely in our home. Together we can make it work.

part 1

Human Aspect of Aging Safely in Your Home — Personal Adaptations

chapter 1

Be Physically Prepared to Age Safely in Your Home

Are you concerned about your health and wellness as you age? Will your ability to remain independent in your home be affected? Are your loved ones concerned for you? Or do you simply assume everything will be fine?

It is easy to overlook the level of physical fitness that is required to age safely in your home, but you need to be prepared for the physical changes that will occur in your future. You might not even consider it if in the past getting around and managing your place was something you did easily. Perhaps you didn't have to think twice about reaching for a vase on the top shelf, moving the lawn mower out of the way, or even reaching for your towel while getting out of the shower. You may have taken for granted your ability to look out the front window to notice who parked across the street. It's possible that a few years ago you quickly responded to the sound of a kettle spouting. When you would get minor cuts or bruises they would heal quickly. As time goes by, your senses and reflexes may not be as sharp. You're probably not as physically strong or agile as you once were.

Physical aging is a gradual process that we may not be aware of until one day we can no longer do something that used to be second nature. How and where we've lived, what cards we've been dealt in terms of genetics, previous injuries and disease also factor into our physical health. Physical aging is natural and inevitable. Virtually every system in our body is affected. To put it simply, the parts are gradually wearing out. Fortunately, it is within your power to slow down and, in some cases, reverse the effects of the aging process. This chapter stresses the importance of playing an active role in your health care and getting regular checkups to gain insight and direction to improve your health.

When parts start to wear out, it is time to adapt our behaviors. The process of adapting to a new level of physical ability can be seen as either a chore or an adventure. It is up to you to choose which attitude will be most helpful when facing your challenges. You may not believe that staying in your own home involves any challenge. The truth is it does take a clear mind and a certain degree of strength, coordination, and vitality to stay in even the most age-friendly home. You don't need to become a senior fitness model, but you do need to be at your best possible level of health in order to maintain independence and be capable of aging safely in your home.

The best possible state of health a person can achieve regardless of his or her individual challenges is described as optimal health. It varies from person to person, and is a moving target that changes with a person's age as well as physical, mental, emotional, and social factors. In my 25 years of clinical practice, the happiest seniors and persons with disabilities are those who constantly adjust to those moving targets with a positive attitude.

Attitude is essential, and there are many things you can do to obtain your optimal level of health at any age. This applies even if you are already at a disadvantage with mobility or other health issues. The degree of challenge will vary from person to person. For example, some of you may already be eating a healthy diet but not exercising. Others may assume they are healthy but have not seen their dentist in two years. Regardless of your starting point, it is always possible to make yourself as healthy as you can be. Do not be discouraged by nature's inevitable way. Aging happens, but there are many factors to physical health that you can have a positive impact on. Having a winning attitude about your physical fitness involves embracing the challenge of making personal adaptions where required, and putting time and energy into achieving your optimal health.

Eating a healthy diet is one of the most important factors that you can control, and may be an area where you need to make personal adaptations. Proper nutrition is important at any age. How well you eat affects how well you age. Section 3 provides a simple visual diagram to help you make wise choices plus some tips for eating healthy.

Other factors that will impact your physical fitness are your ability to manage your medications and pain. The majority of seniors take more than one medication for their various health conditions or to control chronic pain. Chronic pain has been described as a silent epidemic, and this is especially true for seniors. But there is no need to suffer in silence. With proper use of medications and good pain management you can improve your ability to engage in a fulfilling lifestyle. In section 4, you will gain information on how take your medications properly, work with your health-care team to achieve your health goals, and discover techniques to prevent and treat your pain. It is possible to free yourself from pain and have a zest for life!

Getting quality sleep also factors into your physical fitness. Sleep is not an indulgence; your body needs time to rest and recharge. During sleep our bodies regulate hormones that affect the way our cells function. Try following the healthy sleep habits listed in section 6 to get the rest you need to rejuvenate your body.

The question you must ask yourself is: Am I ready to meet the challenge of reaching my optimal health that will allow me to age safely in my home? In this chapter we suggest ways for you to address the physical factors that only you can control. You will learn what is required in order to reach your optimal level of physical health. At the end of the chapter you will find Checklist 1: Rate Yourself: Physical Activity, which you can use to evaluate whether or not you meet the criteria for maintaining your optimal physical health.

1. Get Regular Checkups

Many people believe that the only time to see their doctor is when they're not feeling well. In other words, they view the doctor as a professional who treats illness as opposed to someone who advises them on how to maintain their health and prevent disease.

If you are one of those people, it is time to shift your viewpoint if you wish to age in a healthy manner. Imagine being at the head of a table in a boardroom with your doctor and your other health practitioners. You work together as a health-care team to promote your health and wellness. Your role as the lead team member is to monitor and treat anything that is a barrier to you aging well. Your other team members advise you on the best way to go about this. Your doctor is one of the many health practitioners available to help you achieve optimal health.

Another example would be to think in terms of vehicle maintenance. The driver chooses when to get his or her vehicle serviced. One driver brings her car in for regular check-ups to monitor the brakes, oil, and various operating systems. A different driver waits until his truck's motor isn't functioning well or there's black smoke coming out of the hood. If your body was a vehicle, which driver would you rather have making choices about your maintenance? Just as the black smoke indicates an obvious (and possibly delayed) time to see your mechanic; pain, illness, and low energy are signs (also possibly delayed) that it's time to see your medical doctor.

1.1 Visit your medical doctor

All signs and indicators to seek medical advice are not obvious. There are many health conditions in the body that are "hidden under the surface." Key tests are needed on a regular basis to determine your blood pressure, blood sugar, and cholesterol levels. There may be other tests required based on your individual medical history. If you have not had these tests in the past year, call your doctor's office and request to book in for a full checkup. Your medical doctor will advise you about what you need to do and when to rebook. Aging well physically requires that we know ourselves both inside and out.

1.2 Visit your dentist

Many of us think we only need to see the dentist if we feel there is a cavity. Once again, there is more "hidden under the surface" in oral health, especially in our senior years. Smokers need to be extra vigilant in maintaining oral health, as they are more vulnerable to cavities as well as disease.

As we get older, we enter a second round of cavity-prone years. There are several reasons for this. Our vision is reduced, so we may not see a build-up of plaque or receding gums. Our nerves become less sensitive, so we may not feel the pain or the hot and cold sensitivity that is associated with having a cavity. Our circulation is diminished, so the body cannot repair as quickly. A common side-effect in more than 500 medications is dry mouth, which can cause tooth decay and gum disease. Each one of these factors creates an environment where cavities can rapidly progress. The best advice to prevent oral infection and disease is to see your dentist once every six months.

1.3 Visit your complementary health practitioners

Over the years you may have learned what types of therapies or treatments work best for you. Your health-care team may include Massage Therapists, Naturopathic Doctors, Chiropractors, Physiotherapists, Acupuncturists, or Occupational Therapists (to name a few). Continue to see those professionals who are licensed to treat seniors and their specific issues. Keep your team informed of any changes in your health or medications and never be afraid to let them know if an area is painful or uncomfortable.

2. Exercise Regularly

Exercising may be the most challenging of all the physical criteria for ability to remain at home. Don't despair. Try to maintain a positive attitude by considering this as an adventure not a chore. Keep in mind that exercise can mean anything from consciously stretching and reaching while unloading the dishwasher to running a marathon. The goal is to obtain your optimal physical health while taking into consideration whatever challenges you face.

If you are not already living an active lifestyle, and exercise seems like a lot of effort and work to you; it is time to have a serious talk with yourself. If you are determined to stay at home, then channel some energy into keeping physically fit. Remember your health-team model. Health professionals can only support you by giving advice, but it's up to you to follow their suggestions.

Here are some important reasons you should exercise in order to age safely in your home:

  ✓ Muscular strength will empower you to deal with your day-to-day chores around the house.

  ✓ Coordination and balance are essential to prevent falls. Falling is the number one cause of hospitalization due to injuries in seniors.

✓ Healthy bone density can protect you from serious injuries if you do fall.

✓ Good cardiovascular health will increase your longevity and improve your sense of well-being.

✓ Physical fitness and mental health go hand in hand. Stay fit in body, mind, and spirit. Begin today!

Getting started can be the hardest part, so it's okay to take baby steps in the beginning. Start by informing yourself about the best activities for your age and current level of health. Ask your medical doctor or complementary health practitioner what he or she would advise for you. You can also check with your local community or seniors' center to see if there's a licensed exercise specialist who can advise you about what is available and appropriate for you.

Once you know your options, pick activities that are enjoyable to you. This takes the "chore" out of the equation. Try choosing some activities that make you focus while you do them, as this can create a welcomed mental break from your worries or concerns.

One of my great joys in life is to do exercise that makes me feel I've had a mini-vacation. I sometimes get a bit down during the rainy, gray winter months in Vancouver. The best medicine for me is to take the gondola up Grouse Mountain and go snowshoeing with my friends. High above the clouds and into the bright snow there are often clear skies and beautiful views. Sometimes it's a winter wonderland scene with snow falling. Either way, it's a break from the bleak city weather below the clouds and a way to keep fit while having fun with friends.

Household chores can be considered exercise when done with the intent to improve coordination, strength, and balance. For example, you may be able to unload your dishwasher easily in five minutes. What if you purposely made the most out of the gentle twisting and reaching actions by taking one item at a time instead of handfuls at a time? Stretch out this household activity to fifteen minutes and make it part of your exercise regime for that day.

Participate in an exercise class or do an activity with a friend at least twice per week. Scheduled group exercise may help you stick to a routine as well as provide incentive to participate. You may gain more out of the social aspect of group exercise than doing individual activities. If you prefer individual activities, make sure you vary your exercise by focusing on different activities on different days.

For seniors, daily exercise is more beneficial than infrequent bouts of intense exercise. A half-hour a day of moderate walking, swimming, or raking leaves can reduce the risk of diabetes and heart disease, lower blood pressure, and increase longevity.

Caution: People who are naturally competitive may push themselves too hard, especially when comparing their performance to others in a group setting. The majority of sports-related injuries I treat with massage therapy are caused by patients who have not adequately conditioned their muscles for the intensity of activity they are trying to perform. Keep in mind that your body's flexibility, endurance, and strength naturally decrease with age. Your attitude may need to adapt to new limitations. This doesn't mean "slacking off," but instead altering the intensity or frequency at which you exercise. Build your capacity slowly and gradually in order to attain your optimal fitness without injuries or setbacks.

Do proper gentle stretching before and after each activity to reduce the likelihood of exercise-related pain or injury. Go slow and don't overdo it. Relax into the stretch and breathe deeply. Do not force or try to push the muscles into a length you were once able to attain. Listen to what your body is comfortable with today.

Last, but not least: Be sure to drink plenty of water during and/or after exercise. This is a great way to increase your stamina, flush out toxins, and replenish your fluids.

3. Eat a Healthy Diet

We literally are what we eat. I'm sure you've heard this before. The foods we ingest will fuel our bodies to carry out our every function in life, from breathing, sleeping, and concentrating, to moving around. Having a good diet is essential to keeping ourselves physically fit enough to stay safely at home.

Why is it so hard to implement healthy changes into our diet if we know what fuels are best for us? I believe it is because we are creatures of habit. Year after year we pick the same items and brands from the grocery shelves. We have a repertoire of foods we like and we gravitate towards what's easy to prepare. This is not such a good thing if our choices include a lot of processed foods, or if our selection cannot provide a balanced diet. We may already know what foods we should be eating, yet we choose what is familiar and convenient.

The issue of convenience is a hurdle because eating well takes time. Whole foods such as fruits, vegetables, and grains simply take more time to prepare. Perhaps time management is a factor in your food choices; but investing your time in your own health and nutrition is a wise thing to do.

As a health practitioner I have a clear understanding of the positive effects a good diet has on human function. I am also aware of the consequences of not eating properly, so I choose to make the time to prepare healthy food. If you wish to age safely at home, you will need to make the time to prepare or adjust to a healthy diet. It is never too late to fuel your body properly. Eating better will lead to feeling better.

This diet section explains your best food choices and how to balance them based on the food guides promoted by the World Health Organization. Diagram 1 represents the recommended percentage of portions per daily food intake. Please consult your own country's food guide for suggested daily amounts specific to your age and gender. Also, consult your doctor if you have any condition that requires special diet considerations.

The following include some tips for healthy eating:

- ✓ Save time. Make larger portions of foods that will freeze well and save them for another day. Wash and cut three days' worth of carrot and celery sticks and have them ready and visible in your fridge. Wash whole fruit and vegetables in advance so they are quicker to prepare.

- ✓ Purchase your groceries to reflect the food categories as illustrated in Diagram 1. Dried foods such as grains and legumes can be purchased in larger amounts and stored. Fresh foods such as fruits, vegetables, and dairy products can be bought biweekly or weekly.

- ✓ Liven up your meals by sharing food with guests. Invite friends over and try one new recipe per week. Experiment with different food items. Put a little effort into your table and meal presentation.

- ✓ Try a combination of raw and cooked vegetables. Your ideal meal will have a variety of colors, textures, and flavors.

- ✓ Eat healthy snacks such as fruit, vegetables, nuts, seeds, and whole grain breads and cereals.

Diagram 1
BALANCED MEAL PORTIONS*

Fruits	Grains	Dairy
Whole seasonal fruit is best. Be aware that any prepared fruits, juices, and vegetable salads may have added sugar, salt, and unsaturated fats. Check the food labels before purchasing.	At least half of your grains should be whole grains such as brown rice and whole wheat flour items. Refined grains such as white rice and white flour products can be consumed in smaller amounts.	Drink skim, 1%, or 2% milk or a fortified soy beverage each day. Eat low-fat and low-sugar yogurt, and only small amounts of cheese as part of your dairy intake.

Vegetables	Proteins
Eat a variety of colorful vegetables, with daily servings of dark-green, red, and orange vegetables. Avocados provide a delicious source of unsaturated fats. Sea vegetables such as dulce and kelp contain the highest source of vitamins and minerals and can be lightly sprinkled over salads and in soups.	Only 10 to 15 percent of our daily food intake should contain protein. Select quality lean meat or meat products prepared with little or no added fat or salt. Include seafood, cold-water fish, and eggs into your weekly food plan. Alternate your sources of protein with lentils, soy beans, tofu, black beans, green beans, and mushrooms.

* The My Plate design and website was created by the United States Department of Agriculture (USDA), which can be found at http://www.ChooseMyPlate.gov/.

✓ Avoid overcooking your food. Vegetables can be steamed just enough to make them easier to chew. Stir frying is another great method for cooking food lightly.

✓ Avoid drinking water during a meal. This dilutes enzymes so they cannot break down foods for proper digestion.

✓ Try drinking ginger tea if you need to stimulate your appetite. Cut foods into small pieces and chew slowly.

✓ Minimize the amount of sugared drinks (including alcohol), salts, unsaturated fats, and processed foods you eat.

In addition to following a healthy diet, Canada's Food Guide states that people older than the age of 50 should take a daily vitamin D supplement. If you choose to supplement your diet with any vitamins, be sure to note this on your list of medications.

Important Note: Contact your dentist if your teeth or dentures are causing chewing difficulty. Contact your medical doctor if you have a persistent change in appetite or indigestion.

Golden Rules of Health

1. Quit smoking. It's the best thing you can do to have a positive impact on almost every system in your body. Take action to prevent the many chronic diseases caused by tobacco use. It's never too late to reap the benefits of quitting smoking. There are many support services to help you quit so you can live longer and stronger.

2. Drink water whenever you are thirsty between meals. Drinking lots of pure water each day from a spring, a filtered water source, or even a tap can help to keep your cells hydrated. It is the simplest way to improve health and prevent some of the effects of aging. Your wrinkled skin, brittle bones, aching joints, and dry mouth are crying out for "more WATER"!

---

4. Monitor Your Medications

Keeping yourself physically fit includes being able to manage your medications. You may be one of the substantial numbers of seniors who take multiple medicines daily. Medication for disorders of the heart and circulatory system, digestive system, and respiratory system are commonly used, as are anti-inflammatories, pain relievers, and antidepressants, just to name a few. The more drugs a person takes the greater the chance of experiencing side effects. Caring for yourself properly includes keeping a current record of your medications as well as any other supplements you are taking. Have your medications reviewed from time to time and always verify that any new medications are compatible with what you are already taking.

In order to keep track of your medications, sort them out in advance. Using day-of-the-week or color-coded pillboxes may help you keep track of timing. For example, a yellow daily pillbox left near the fridge may contain certain medications to be taken in the morning, while having a black daily pillbox left on the kitchen table may contain medications that need to be taken in the afternoon or evening. You can also use labels or stickers with specific written instructions or reminders to help you keep track.

When you do take your medications, be sure to take them as directed. Improper use of medications can cause disorientation, dizziness, and poisoning, all of which put seniors at risk of injury and illness. Some pills are meant to be taken with meals, others without. Some pills are meant to be taken at certain times of the day. It can get confusing trying to keep track, especially with multiple medications, so you need an organizational system that works for you.

I've had patients, young and old who were not wise consumers of their medications. The majority of this group did not have a list recording what they were taking. Some of them said they were only guessing at why the medication needed to be taken. Others were aware of having side effects, but didn't know which medication might be causing them. They had never thought of taking on an active role in their own health care.

Always remember that you play the leading role in your own health-care team that works together to bring you to optimal health and wellness. Have a discussion with your team members regarding the least amount of medications that will provide the best results for your condition. Be informed about what you are taking, why you need it, and how to take it properly. Read the medication pamphlets and let your health-care team know if you are experiencing any side effects. Getting your medications right is a moving and changing target that needs regular monitoring to hit the bullseye.

5. Manage Your Pain

Chronic pain is something many seniors live with. Unfortunately this can become a barrier to aging well if it prevents seniors from getting exercise, socializing, or engaging in a fulfilling lifestyle. This can lead to physical isolation and depression. Chronic pain affects not only our physical body, but our mind and spirit as well. Seniors are among the largest group that suffers from inadequate pain control. They tend to minimize the pain, and are sometimes unable to effectively communicate their symptoms. Their liver and kidney function has decreased, so medications are not processed as effectively. Sadly, sometimes their complaints of pain are dismissed or overlooked.

It is not wise to suffer with pain. Describe the pain to your physician and ask for treatment. Pain management is crucial to achieving your optimal health. Make sure your comments have been heard and are being addressed. Remember, in order to age safely in your home, you need to play the lead role in your health-care team by reporting your symptoms and being active in your own health and wellness treatments.

You may be familiar with the saying "An ounce of prevention is worth a pound of cure." This applies particularly well to any chronic pain associated with physical aging. As mentioned earlier, our physical parts wear down as we age and we are not capable of bouncing back from injuries as quickly as we once did. Because of this, we must be extra careful to prevent any painful situations. Getting regular checkups, exercising at a level appropriate for you, eating a well-balanced diet, and drinking plenty of water can significantly prevent or decrease pain.

In order to prevent injuries or aggravating chronic pain, I would advise you to pace yourself. This may be tougher than it sounds if your mindset has not adapted from previous decades and you are still comparing what you could do in the past to what you are capable of doing now. Do yourself a favor and learn to work at a slower pace and rest when you need to. It is better to avoid a painful situation due to overuse than to suffer the consequences. We simply do not "bounce back" as quickly as we used to, so adopt a preventive attitude for managing your pain.

Another significant contributor to pain is stress. If you are already living a healthy lifestyle yet feel there is more you might be able to do to manage your chronic pain, ask yourself, "How am I dealing with the stress in my life?" Fortunately, stress management is a factor that is within our control, and will be discussed in Chapter 3.

When you are in pain it may seem more comfortable to just stay at home. Studies show that people who cut themselves off from their social circles are more likely to become depressed and are less able to manage their illness. Stay involved with your family, friends, and social activities. Be aware of your behavior around managing pain. If you are reducing your social activities because of the pain you are experiencing, be sure to report this to your health-care team because there are solutions.

There are many simple, cost-effective treatments for pain. Arthritis and chronic back pain may be relieved by applying warm packs to the affected area, or soaking hands or feet in warm water. Other conditions may respond well to postural changes and specific resting positions. Ask your physician or certified-health practitioner about the best home remedies for your condition.

I have been so humbled in my clinical practice to learn from my patients who play an active role in their health, especially with those who are dealing with chronic pain. As I've mentioned before, they have inspired me by constantly adapting to their condition with a positive attitude. They have shown me that some of the simplest pain-management techniques come in the form of drinking plenty of water, keeping warm, pacing themselves, and using the therapies and resting positions that work best for their conditions.

6. Get Quality Sleep

There's a magical, restoring power to sleep! Is that a thing of the past for you? If you are getting less than six hours of sleep per night, you may be experiencing decreased alertness, concentration, or libido. You may become more forgetful, get cravings for sweets and carbohydrates, have dark circles under your eyes, or feel depressed. If so, there are personal adaptations that you can make to help you get a good night's rest on a more consistent basis.

Many elderly people suffer from a variety of disorders that can, and do, disrupt sleep. Among them are arthritis, heartburn, incontinence, gastro-esophageal reflux, cardiovascular disease, and dementia. All of these conditions can interrupt, delay, and/or shorten sleep. Elderly people generally secrete lower amounts of chemicals that regulate the sleep/wake cycle. In addition, reduced exposure to sunlight and a decrease in exercise and mental stimulation, plus a changed diet, may increase sleep difficulties. It may also be difficult to obtain quality sleep at night if you are grieving or taking medications with side effects of insomnia.

Managing sleep patterns can be a real challenge. I've heard my elderly patients say the toughest part for them is avoiding daytime naps or falling asleep in front of the television. My advice for preventing napping is to schedule a walk or another activity just before that time of day. The same can be done to prevent falling asleep in front of the television. Consult your health-care team if none of the following techniques to manage your sleep are effective:

✓ Maintain a regular waking and bed time.

✓ Decrease or eliminate daytime naps.

- ✓ Exercise daily, but not immediately before going to bed.
- ✓ Avoid heavy snacks, alcohol, caffeine, and nicotine before bedtime.
- ✓ Get adequate exposure to bright light during the day.
- ✓ Wind down before going to bed.
- ✓ Sleep in a cool, quiet, dark room.

7. Rate Yourself: Physical Activity

Checklist 1 will help you evaluate whether or not you meet the criteria for obtaining your optimal physical health and independence to age safely in your home. Apply the information to your current habits, not what you might consider changing. Using a pencil, check your answers. If any of your answers are "no," read the corresponding information in this chapter for suggestions on how to make it a "yes." If the challenges are still too overwhelming, this is the time to consider moving to a more suitable living situation.

Checklist 1
RATE YOURSELF: PHYSICAL ACTIVITY

Physical Activity	Yes	No
Regular checkups with your medical doctor.		
Regular checkups with your dentist.		
Visits to your complementary health practitioners.		
Cardiovascular exercise two to three times per week.		
Strength, balance, and coordination activities two to three times per week.		
Meals contain mostly fruits, vegetables, and grains.		
Only a *small* amount of the food or drinks you consume are processed or have a high sugar, saturated fat, or salt content.		
Drinking plenty of water during the day.		
Medications regularly reviewed and taken on time.		
Pain is being well-managed.		
Six to eight hours of sleep per night.		
Quitting smoking (for smokers only).		

chapter 2

Maintain an Active Social Network

Is your home the same bustling center of activity it once was? Are there a mixture of young and old, friends, family, and guests going through your doors? Do you leave the house for work, shopping, and social activities as often as before? Are you getting the charge you need from being around other people?

It is likely your social circle has gradually dwindled both within and outside of your home. Depending on your life circumstances, this could mean the loss of a spouse or that your children have moved along. It may be that some of your friends have become more physically isolated or have even passed away. You may simply be slowing down and don't feel like being around people as often. These circumstances can lead to social isolation.

Social isolation is one of the barriers to aging well. Although our physical bodies do naturally "wear down," our social, mental, emotional, and spiritual health are factors that are much more under our personal control. These factors do have a significant effect on our physical health. Numerous studies have shown that people who maintain social connections with a wide variety of social networks live longer, have stronger immune systems, and maintain better mental health.

Human beings are social creatures who once lived in tribes with strong community connections. Times have changed. These days we need to define, find, and maintain a tribe that helps us live day to day. We need to seek support from our tribe. Without the support from our tribe, the normal aging process involves a narrowing social network, a growing dependence on others, and increasing isolation and loneliness. It doesn't have to be this way! Regardless of your age or your current social network, it is entirely possible to overcome social isolation by staying connected or finding connection in your own community.

In chapter one, your visual tool for overcoming barriers to physical aging is to envision yourself as the lead member in the boardroom of your health-care team. Now I'd like you to imagine yourself at the center of your own tribe. Each member works towards keeping the entire tribe functioning at its best. In order for this to work, each member contributes to helping the others as well as graciously receiving and accepting help from others. Are you able to imagine being part of a tribe that works towards helping you age safely in your home?

The bottom line is it will take a team effort for you to remain safely in your home, whether you are single or living with a spouse, other family member, or friend. The effort on your part involves the following:

✓ Creating or maintaining an active social network.

✓ Being active in your community.

✓ Accepting adequate home care and support.

This chapter will help you to evaluate the social challenges you may face and how to broaden your social network. It also provides a useful guideline to asking for and gaining support.

It may be discouraging to know that you need help from others. If you can visualize the tribal model, you will understand that others need help from you as well. Perhaps it will be easier for you to accept help if you know that you are also contributing to the well-being of others. There are many fulfilling ways for you to use this time in your life to "give back" to the tribe that you have created. In order for a tribe to coexist in a healthy manner, members must be able to communicate their needs. Asking for help may be a challenge for you, but is a skill you can achieve with practice.

Accessing social activities outside the home may become more difficult as you age. Just as people plan ahead for retirement, they should also think about their plan for transportation as they grow older. There will likely come a time when it is wise to retire from driving and use alternate sources of transportation. This chapter explains the importance of knowing when to retire from driving, and how to prevent social isolation when you are no longer driving. If you plan to age safely in your home, you must also plan to travel safely outside your home.

For many seniors the issue of social isolation is not due to lack of desire to connect with people; it is often due to difficulty in accessing others. Fortunately, technology has provided us with a multitude of ways to socialize. It's never too late to learn how to use a computer or other device to help you connect with people. We encourage you to use technology to build and enrich your social connections.

1. Keep in Close Touch with Your Innermost Circle

The innermost circle of a traditional tribe extends beyond one's immediate family. You may currently be living with a spouse or other family member. While this may be ideal for you, many individuals tend to rely heavily on the person they are living with for reassurance and assistance when needed.

As you age, the burden of maintaining your health and home will naturally increase. Keeping only a small social circle can place an increasing stress on those individuals who are closest to you. It is wise to expand your tribe beyond your innermost circle. Not only will the burden be shared, but you will gain a fresh perspective from being around a variety of individuals.

If you have no family, or you are estranged from some of them, you will need to redefine your innermost circle to include your closest friends or neighbors. Keep in touch with individuals in this group on a regular basis to socialize or even just to touch base and keep them informed on how you're doing. If you are living alone and your current state of health and mobility puts you at risk for falls, you should be checking in with someone on a daily basis. Having a close circle to check in with is important for making sure you are safe and well.

Fewer seniors are living in large extended family communities where their roles are clearly defined and guided by the needs of the younger members. The role you wish to play as an elder in your own tribe is for you to envision and create. Think about how you would like to be involved with your family and friends and discuss with them what will work best.

Make contact with your innermost circle by phone or in person on a regular basis. Show genuine interest for them by asking how they are doing and what is new in their home, work, and social lives. Don't forget that the people in your circle love you and want to know how things are going for you. Keep them posted on what is new in your life and make time to share your stories.

If you have grandchildren or other young people you would like to see more of, offer to babysit. Chasing after children is a fun way to keep physically active and improve your sense of well-being. If this sounds like too much work, but you still enjoy being around children, choose an easier activity such as taking them to one of their various sporting or leisure activities. There are many ways to contribute to their lives in a meaningful way. Choose to be involved in the way that works for you.

Scheduling a family dinner is a great way to keep connected. Meal times have traditionally been social affairs; a time to share not only food, but also news, ideas, feelings, fun, and conversation. If preparing large meals is no longer of interest to you, suggest you meet for dessert or predinner appetizers or coordinate a potluck dinner. Plan ahead for the holidays, and consider traveling to distant relatives on a rotating basis with your closer family members. The most important thing is to know there are many ways to stay connected to your innermost circle.

2. Be Actively Involved in Your Local Community

Our nearest geographical tribal members are our neighbors. In tribal living, we relied on those members to contribute to the well-being and survival of the group. Now our social contacts are spread far and wide, and it is not uncommon for many of us to regard our own neighbors as strangers. Take a moment to envision your location and the tribe that live in your neighborhood. Ask yourself: "Who are my neighbors? Why are they important to me? How do I contribute to their lives?"

Living in a place where you have helpful and trustworthy neighbors will enable you to feel more comfortable and secure. This can promote a willingness to walk through your neighborhood to either get to the places you need to go or to exercise outside of your home. Having this "neighborhood security" can encourage you to stay mobile and maintain your independence. Some of your closest neighbors may even become a part of your extended family or your innermost social circle.

Creating this extended family might seem like a strange idea or make you feel uncomfortable. Remember that having a strong social network is crucial to maintaining your health and wellness. It's an important piece of the "aging safely" puzzle, and it's up to you to ensure that all of the pieces of the puzzle are completed.

2.1 Tips to expand your community network

If you wish to expand your social network and are living in an apartment, consider getting involved in the social aspect of that community. Here are a few tips to help you meet and connect with your neighbors:

- ✓ Post an invitation to begin a book club, card club, or other weekly activity.
- ✓ Take advantage of your building's community room to host a luncheon.
- ✓ Offer to take your neighbor's dog for a walk or to cat-sit while the person is away.
- ✓ Get involved in the building's strata council or join a special interest group in the building or community.
- ✓ Initiate a "building party" around a seasonal event.
- ✓ Start a walking or running group.

Regardless of where you live, there are many ways to get to know your neighbors. During the past few summers I've seen many block parties where neighbors obtain a permit to close their street to traffic and organize a BBQ. Young and old, families and singles share food, play games, dance, and celebrate. It's a fun way to get to know each other to build strong community alliances and neighborhood security. Perhaps this is one way for you to bring your own neighborhood closer together.

Beyond your immediate neighbors are your extended community members. Every new connection you make through your community has the potential to become an active part of your social network. Spending time at activity centers and community events will help you build connections and relationships with people nearby.

Community and seniors' centers offer a wide variety of programs and classes that may interest you. Many of these programs involve activities to keep you fit while others are less physical and involve more mental stimulation. Some centers host support groups that are related to a physical condition or illness you may have. Others offer group meals at reasonable prices. Find out what your local community or seniors' center has to offer and expand your social circle to include the new friends you make there.

On a personal note, I've had to expand my social network as new aches, pains, and physical changes have come upon me in my 50s. This year I will not be able to keep up with my friends in our fast-paced snowshoe group. I hate to admit it, but I'm not happy being the straggler at the back of the pack! One option is to quit the activity altogether. The other is to expand my social network by joining the "leisure group" even though I don't know anyone. For me, it will be worth the initial discomfort of breaking away from my familiar group of friends in order to meet new people who share my enjoyment of the outdoors.

3. Ask for the Help You Need

Asking for help is difficult for most of us because we see it as a sign of weakness. We tend to overlook the fact that we are all social beings that need to cooperate with one another in order to thrive. Learning to ask for help is a social skill that we all need. In the case of seniors, it is a required skill in order to age safely in their home.

To develop this social skill you first need to think of the reasons why it is hard for you to ask for help. It may be hard to swallow your pride if you cannot solve a problem, or you're no longer capable of "fixing" an item. Ask yourself if this pride is of any benefit to you or others. Are you better off to suffer in silence rather than admitting that you need help? It will build your own strength of character to simply acknowledge that there is something you need help with today. Just like other people, from time to time you need help, and that's ok. Try to focus on the big picture: Your tribe that thrives on human cooperation. Imagine how good it feels to you when you are able to help others. Give people a chance to do the same for you.

Once you've gotten into a more positive frame of mind about asking for help, prioritize your needs and ask someone you trust. You will enable this person to assist you by being specific about what you need help with. It makes his or her job easier to do, or to find someone else who has the expertise or time required.

The next skill is to accept the help you've asked for. Work on overcoming any negative feelings associated with needing help, and remember that you too contribute to your tribe. Give to others and know that you are worthy of receiving help as well. Finally, show your gratitude. No dramatics needed! A simple "thank you" goes a long way.

3.1 Things you may need help with

There are many things you may need help with if you choose to remain in your home. Some items that you may wish to ask for help from your innermost circle include the following:

- ✓ Preparing meals, paying bills, and shopping.
- ✓ Taking out the garbage, raking leaves, or shoveling snow.
- ✓ Transporting you to outings.
- ✓ Joining you during important meetings with professionals.
- ✓ Doing home safety checks or vehicle and house maintenance.

3.2 Where to find the help you need

There are countless sources of help once you decide to ask for what you need. Distant family members and friends may have offered their help but didn't know exactly how to be of assistance. Be as specific as possible when asking for help.

Some things they might be happy to do for you include:

- ✓ Organizing online bill payments.
- ✓ Doing research required for getting home care or house renovations done.
- ✓ Keeping you "in the loop" by sending you video clips or photographs of their current events.

Some of your neighbors may be willing to keep an eye on your place while you're away, help you with heavy groceries, drive you to appointments, or research local activities and services.

Younger adults who live in your area might enjoy helping with seasonal chores such as shoveling snow, raking leaves, or weeding.

Seek help from your extended community. Senior and community centers employ workers who can assist you in gaining information regarding your interests and needs. They may be able to connect you with appropriate volunteer services. Help is out there; you only need to ask.

3.3 Obtaining emergency help

Most of us feel strong, capable, and safe until we are proven otherwise. It is often the case for the children of seniors to be more concerned about their parents' decline in hearing, strength, and balance than the seniors are for themselves.

Your loved ones have very rational worries about you hurting yourself if you fall at home and they are not there to help you. If you are a senior who is planning to remain in your home for as long as possible, you must take a proactive approach to falls and the assistance you may eventually need. This is especially true if you are living alone or with someone who is not capable or properly trained to help you. You must be prepared for the possibility of not being able to access your telephone for emergency assistance.

Now is the time to discuss the safety options you may need even if you feel it is not necessary at this point. Ask for help to research the various medical alert systems (e.g., Lifeline) that you could access by pressing a button on a wristband or pendant. You'll ease your loved one's concerns and be more secure in your home because emergency help will always be available.

4. Use Transportation Options

Access to social contacts, shopping, activity centers, and medical services is very important to seniors. In fact, it is one of the main reasons why seniors choose to relocate.

If you wish to age safely in a home that is not close to amenities and social contacts, you need to consider what transportation options are available to you. If you currently drive, it is not wise to assume you will be able to continue driving safely forever.

Our senses become diminished as a natural part of aging. Think about how much you need your vision, hearing, touch, and even smell when you drive. Mentally, our complex problem-solving abilities, memory, and judgment decrease. Physically, we lose strength, flexibility, and fluidity of movement. All of these factors tend to slow down our reaction time. Clearly, our ability to drive safely is a serious issue that needs to be dealt with before an accident occurs.

Our egos can trick us into thinking we are still capable of driving even when we've reached the point that it is unsafe to continue. Be aware of becoming less confident and more agitated or confused when you're driving. Listen to your passengers' concerns. Get regular checkups with your health-care team to help you determine your ability to drive. The decision to retire from driving could add valuable years to your life, prevent serious injuries, and enable you to age safely in your home.

Checklist 2
DRIVING SAFELY*

Diminished Driving Skills	Never	Sometimes	Often
Difficulty turning to see when backing up.			
Easily distracted while driving.			
Incorrect signaling.			
Difficulty parking within a defined space.			
Getting scrapes or dents on the vehicle or in the garage.			
Failure to notice important roadside activity and signage.			
Driving at inappropriate speeds (e.g., too fast, too slow).			
Delayed response to unexpected situations.			
Difficulty maintaining lane position.			
Confusion at exits.			
Failure to stop at a stop sign or red light.			
Confusing the brake pedal for the gas pedal, or vice versa.			
Stopping in traffic for no apparent reason.			

*Source: Information provided in Checklist 2 was inspired by the Canadian Initiative for Elder Planning Studies.

Retiring from driving can be one of the most difficult choices or requirements a senior may need to make. Many people consider their vehicle as their most valued form of independence, mobility, and freedom. Understandably, these people are very reluctant to give up their car keys. Unfortunately seniors who are in denial about their decreased driving abilities are often involved in serious vehicle accidents.

Studies show that senior citizen drivers have the highest fatality rate in vehicle accidents. This is partly because of the severity of the crashes, but also because the frailty that comes from age makes it much more difficult to recover from the physical trauma of a vehicle accident. Retiring from driving may be difficult but for most of us it will be necessary at some point.

The good news is there are many ways to preserve your independence without driving your own vehicle. Prepare to retire from driving by getting to know your transportation options. You may wish to have a discussion with someone in your innermost circle about various ways you can get to your shopping, appointments, and activities. It may be easy for friends that attend the same functions to provide a ride.

Contact your local bus service and ask about the routes that serve you. Inquire at your local seniors' center about any transportation programs that may be available. If you have a favorite taxicab driver, or someone can recommend one, get a business card and use his or her services to deliver you in a timely manner.

You don't need to be the driver in order to be mobile. Ultimately, you may learn to enjoy the view instead of concentrating on the road. What you do need is to be able to access your amenities and social activities.

5. Use Technology to Build Your Social Connections

If you wish to enhance your social network, the computer age has made it possible to virtually connect with people almost anywhere on the planet! There are many tools that can bring you closer to your distant relatives and friends. If you do not already use email or social media, such as Facebook, Skype, or FaceTime, you may be missing out on a wonderful way to connect with your loved ones.

Learning to use a computer is daunting to many seniors who fear it is too complicated. However, there are countless seniors in their 70s, 80s, and 90s who would beg to differ. The hesitance to learn new skills is common for someone whose vision, hearing, and dexterity have decreased over time. Fortunately there are simple solutions that address the needs of seniors who are new to computing. Age-friendly software programs make your computer easier to see, hear, and interact with. It's not as complicated as you think.

Take the first step toward learning about computers by researching software programs for seniors. Ask for assistance from someone in your tribe to help you with this. It could be an opportunity for someone to assist you in a way that is fun and meaningful for him or her. You'd be amazed by the enthusiasm and savvy that many young people have regarding computers and social media. Ask the person to narrow down a few options then decide together which one is best for you.

Some people find it easier to learn one-on-one from a person who is a close social connection. Others gain more from joining a class in their community and being around other beginners. Whatever method you choose, make sure that you will be able to get support during your learning curve over the next few weeks. An amazing new world will be at your fingertips.

For those of you who are already comfortable with computer use, you may wish to challenge yourself to learn what new communication methods your grandkids or younger friends are using. Ask them if they'd like to teach you the best or newest way for you to connect with them. You may be surprised at how quickly they respond!

The other day I was thrilled to hear the story of a friend of mine who'd gone overseas on holidays with her sister and mother. The two sisters were having problems in this foreign country with their Internet and wireless connections. Their 75-year-old mother had learned to use computers before she retired and was able to solve her daughters' technological problems as well as keep the rest of the family in contact during the vacation by writing group emails and sending photos along the way! I'm hoping that once you become familiar with a few social media programs you will also be inspired to be the hub of your online community

6. Rate Yourself: Social Activity

Checklist 3 will help you evaluate whether or not you meet the criteria for obtaining your optimal social health and independence to age safely in your home. Apply the information to your current habits, not what you might consider changing. Using a pencil, check your answers. If any of your answers are "no," read the corresponding information in this chapter for suggestions on how to make them a "yes." If the challenges are still too overwhelming, this is the time to consider moving to a more suitable living situation.

Checklist 3
RATE YOURSELF: SOCIAL ACTIVITY

Social Activity	Yes	No
Frequent phone calls or visits with people in your innermost circle.		
Daily contact with someone if you have a tendency to fall.		
Eat a meal with others frequently.		
Exercise or do activities with others at least twice per week.		
Be on good terms with at least two neighbors.		
Attend an event or do an activity at your nearest seniors' center or community location at least every second week.		
Be able to ask for help from someone you trust with housing, transportation, or other issues when needed.		
Have access to and utilize safe transportation methods.		
Have a communication system that lets others know you are safe and well.		

chapter 3

Be Emotionally Happy in Your Home

Do you fear getting older alone? Are you grieving the loss of friends or relatives? Are you anxious about your finances or your own personal security? Do you have the emotional capacity to face the challenges of your ever-changing circumstances? These questions may weigh heavily on your mind and affect your emotional state, which leads to undue stress. This undue stress can be highly detrimental to your physical and mental health.

There is no need for most people to fear getting older. Most of those fears stem from myths about aging that are exaggerated by the media or are simply untrue. Many of the once disabling problems of aging can be coped with through improved lifestyle choices, health care, and the use of assisting devices and services.

The truth is that you are stronger and more resilient than you may think. Rest assured that if you are willing to make the personal and housing adaptations listed in Part 2, you will be empowered to have a full, rich, and long life in your own home.

Seniors who are emotionally healthy are able to handle life's many challenges, build strong relationships, and recover from setbacks. But just as it requires effort to build or maintain physical health, so it is with mental and emotional health. If you can balance your sense of loss with positive ingredients, you have a formula for staying mentally and emotionally healthy as you age. This balance will benefit all aspects of your life, including boosting your mood, building resilience, and adding to your overall vitality.

Positive ingredients that bring you to emotional balance include any healthy coping habits that help you deal with life's inevitable stress. Healthy coping habits begin with honest self-assessment in order to recognize your own feelings. Next, you need to take positive action in order to reduce your stress and return to a more balanced emotional state. This will be a continuous and ongoing cycle.

This chapter provides a flow chart (see Diagram 2) that illustrates how to recognize emotional stress and helps you take action. You will have many opportunities to choose which path you will follow. Choosing good coping habits is the best way to add positive ingredients to the formula for reducing your stress.

Another positive ingredient in this formula is to reduce your stress about your finances and your future. One of the most common concerns for people is the issue of financial security. It affects our emotional state at every stage in life, and particularly for seniors who are no longer employed. In order to help keep you in emotional balance, we've included a guideline to address your finances, health care, and estate planning.

The issue of personal safety can also be a great stressor to seniors who are feeling more vulnerable as they age. Prevention is the key ingredient needed in this formula. Follow the list of valuable safety tips provided to help protect yourself and your property.

In order to achieve a healthy emotional state, you may need to make several personal adaptations in the way you prevent and deal with stress. Major life changes happen frequently to seniors whether we want them to or not. How you handle those changes is the key to living a life without undue emotional stress. There are also some tips on how to open your heart to change so you will find ways to turn the unexpected into an opportunity for growth.

1. Acknowledge Your Feelings

Feelings of depression, anxiety, grief, and loneliness are normal reactions to major life changes. Healthy, active seniors routinely adjust to the dramatic changes and challenges associated with aging. The best way to deal with strong emotions that do come up is to first recognize them; then make healthy choices that will help you cope with your situation. Diagram 2 illustrates how to recognize emotional stress then take action that will enable you to age safely in your home.

Diagram 2
RECOGNIZE AND DEAL WITH EMOTIONAL STRESS*

Anxiety	Grief
Excessive fear or worrying. Poor sleep habits. May also suffer from panic, compulsive, hoarding, or other disorders.	Overwhelming emotions that can cause anger, loneliness, depression, guilt, sorrow, fear, and anxiety.
Depression	**Loneliness**
Persistent sadness. Lack of energy or interest in things that were once enjoyable. Frequent tearfulness. Weight changes. Changes in sleep patterns. Inability to concentrate. Irritability and intolerance.	Persistent sense of feeling alone regardless of human interaction. Feeling of being unworthy of attention. Feeling unwanted by others. Feeling isolated despite being around others. Feeling like there's nobody to confide in.

Take Action

Poor Coping Habits	Good Coping Habits
Minimize the problem. Hide the emotions. Pretend you're OK. Avoid social contact. Avoid physical activities. Self-medicate with drugs or alcohol. Stay busy in order to avoid your feelings.	Recognize and address emotions or behaviors. Talk with a trusted confidant in your innermost social circle. Seek advice from members of your health-care team. Keep physically, mentally, and socially active.

Increase your risk of illness. Decrease your ability to remain safely in your home.   **Age safely in your home.**

*This chart shows only generalized symptoms and is not to be used as a diagnostic tool.

1.1 Tips for managing stress

You may think there is very little you can do to control the external factors that add to your stress. In fact, managing stress is all about taking charge of your thoughts and how you deal with the various problems and losses that affect you. Use Diagram 2 to help you recognize your emotional stress and identify the way you are dealing with your stress. Consider using these additional good coping habits:

- ✓ **Avoid stressors:** Avoid the people or topics that aggravate you. Learn to say "no" to avoid feeling overwhelmed. Distinguish between things you "should do" and those you "must do." Turn off the news or other programs that depress you.

- ✓ **Take account of the things that make you grateful:** Focus on the present moment and the simple things that add value to your life now. Cherish your good memories and avoid dwelling on the bad.

- ✓ **Accept the things you can't change:** Concentrate on your ability to bounce back and find positive ways to look at the circumstances you can't change.

- ✓ **Learn to forgive:** Accept the fact that we are imperfect beings in an imperfect world. Show compassion to yourself and others for mistakes that have been made.

- ✓ **Look for the silver lining:** Congratulate yourself for your achievements and the challenges you have already overcome in life. Consider the personal growth you've experienced as a result of coping with a stressful situation.

- ✓ **Use humor to cope:** Look for humor in daily life. Learn to laugh at yourself. Make time for activities or TV shows that make you laugh out loud.

2. Secure Your Future

Long and fruitful senior years at home are not the only product of good health and strong social networks; your emotional well-being is also necessary. As you know, stress plays heavily into your emotional as well as your physical health.

Major stressors that must be taken into consideration involve your financial security and future direction. By addressing these items you will reduce considerable stress for yourself and those who care about your well-being. Although the very idea of calculating expenses or filing formal documents may not appeal to you, feelings of lingering worry or guilt may harbor inside you until the job is completed. It's not worth the added stress to ignore these issues.

If you're anything like me, dealing with finances is a necessary burden. Year after year I sit down to prepare my income tax bookkeeping with the same feeling of dread and drudgery. I tend to make a mountain out of a mole hill when it comes to thinking about the body of work in front of me. The funny thing is, year after year I surprise myself at how little time it actually requires to complete the job. The payoff is the feeling of relief and accomplishment once it's done.

2.1 Financial planning

Having a financial plan and documenting your wishes is necessary for obtaining peace of mind and a sustainable lifestyle. When the time comes to create or revise your long-term financial plan, it is advisable to obtain help from a trusted professional who can guide you through this process. A professional can help you determine your goals, maximize on your income tax deductions, and advise you on making the best use of your assets. Long-term financial planning that involves aging safely in your home will take a considerable amount of time, effort, and expertise. Consulting a professional will reduce the burden on you and will give you a clear picture of where you stand financially. You'll be able to explain this advice to your loved ones and involve them in your future direction if you wish. You may even ask them to join you in your consultation with your financial planner.

One common assumption is that staying in your own home will be less expensive than paying for residential care. While that may be true for some people, it depends on their circumstances and whether they have accounted for the required personal and housing adaptation factors mentioned in this book. When making your long-term financial plan, be sure to budget for the likely probability of needing home adaptations, renovations, and home-care support. Your long-term financial plan will help you assess your financial ability to age safely at home.

2.2 Estate planning: Last will and testament

Your estate is part of your legacy, so it is wise to make formal arrangements to convey how and when you'd like your estate to be utilized and protected while you are still living. If you have not created an estate plan, begin now to consider your property and explore the best ways to meet your current goals.

Estate planning may not start with a will, but it always ends up with writing a last will and testament. Many seniors have already written their will in order to clarify what will happen to their estate when they die. If you are not one of these people, it is time to get the job done. You will spare your loved ones the responsibility of making difficult decisions, there will be fewer fees and delays, and you may even gain some peace of mind.

The question to ask is, "How do I wish to distribute my wealth after death?" This question requires careful thought and informed planning. Once you have established who should benefit from your wealth, you want to transfer it to them with the lowest possible tax bill. Having your estate planning and last will completed with the help of a financial professional can reduce your stress and anxiety levels about securing the near and long-term future.

2.3 Living wills and advance health-care directives

Although many seniors have written a last will, far fewer have documented their wishes for their health care and finances should they become incapacitated while still living. Many people assume they will always be well enough to speak for themselves, or that their loved ones will know how to act for them should they fall under disabling circumstances. Unfortunately, this is not always the case.

Although we are not able to be in complete control of our future, there are ways to maintain our autonomy. It is our right to have a say in our ongoing lifestyle and health care. Our values and personal wishes for the future need to be properly documented in order to have a clear plan for others to refer to should we become incapable of acting on our own behalf. Proper documentation such as a living will can be referred to when you are unconscious or mentally incapacitated. It can also clarify direction and ensure adherence even when you are still able to speak on your own behalf.

Depending on where you live, valid documents that express your health-care wishes may be called a Living Will, an Advanced Directive, or an Advanced Health-Care Directive. It may need to be accompanied by an Enduring Power of Attorney or a Representation Agreement. Terminology in legal documents will vary from place to place. Laws differ greatly between countries and often within regions of the same country. For these and many other reasons it is necessary to consult a legal professional for appropriate filing. Secure your health-care autonomy by completing the documents that are required and valid in your jurisdiction.

3. Protect Yourself

Do you feel more vulnerable to criminal activity as you are getting older? While seniors can be targets of crime, don't let the fear of crime stop you from enjoying life. Prevention is the key ingredient, so ease your worries by protecting yourself. It is possible to reduce your risk of becoming a target by following these personal safety tips:

- ✓ Know your neighbors and be involved in an active Neighborhood Watch Program.
- ✓ Do not give out personal information over the phone or in an email.
- ✓ Protect your passwords and keep computer security software up to date.
- ✓ Walk with your head up and be alert.
- ✓ Carry a cell phone for emergency calls.
- ✓ Avoid walking in darkness or unlit areas. Walk with a friend.
- ✓ Avoid carrying or keeping large amounts of money on your person or at home.
- ✓ Park in well-lit areas and do not open your door or roll down your window for a stranger.
- ✓ Never resist a robber. Hand over your purse or wallet without a fight.
- ✓ Report elder abuse. Call police and ask for the Elder Protection service.

4. Open Your Heart to Change

Over the years you have undoubtedly experienced many highs and lows. Our formula of balancing those lows with positive ingredients may present a challenge for you. It requires an open heart and an open mind.

You may find yourself resisting change. You might not want to install a handrail at your front steps, or make new friends in your neighborhood. You may find reasons to avoid engaging in social activities or to delay your financial planning. Unfortunately seniors must constantly adapt to the inevitable changes in their health, mobility, and social lives. How you adapt to these changes will determine your success in overcoming the barriers to aging well.

The next time you are faced with a challenging life decision, consider the positive outcomes for adapting to your new circumstances. Your ability to adapt to change will empower you to age safely in your home. On an emotional level you will be happier, more content, more relaxed, less stressed, and less lonely. You will be actively engaged in your life and able to contribute more to others.

4.1 Tips for adapting to change

If the idea of change is still difficult for you, here are some tips to help you along the way:

- ✓ Envision the positive benefits of making the changes that will empower you.

- ✓ Be aware of your excuses and free up some time to make changes.

- ✓ Gain inspiration from seniors who you admire for their resiliency and vitality.

- ✓ Involve others; listen to their suggestions and accept their help.

- ✓ Make changes at a pace that is comfortable for you and shows progress.

- ✓ Be patient with yourself and give changes a chance to provide results.

I have recently had to make a major life change because of a shoulder injury that rendered me incapable of working. For 25 years I'd had an enjoyable and fulfilling career as a Registered Massage Therapist. I truly loved my job and the wonderful patients I'd gotten to know over the years. I felt I could have gone on until retirement in this line of work. Unfortunately, my physical self could not keep up. Massage therapy is highly demanding physical labor, and my body had been giving me signals that it was growing weary. After a period of feeling sorry for myself and grieving the loss of a career I loved, I set out to discover what possibilities lay ahead. In order to do so, I had to accept my situation and learn how to apply my values and interests to a new job description. This was a humbling and challenging endeavor that required I open my heart and adapt to my physical limitations. Now I have built a new career as a Dementia Care Educator and Elder Planning Counselor. It is a wonderful and meaningful occupation that I may not have discovered unless I'd had those physical ailments. The work is much less physically draining, yet equally as rewarding. It's been the silver lining in what seemed to be a dark cloud of change.

5. Rate Yourself: Emotional Activity

Checklist 4 will help you evaluate whether or not you meet the criteria for obtaining your optimal emotional health and independence to age safely in your home. Apply the information to your current habits, not what you might consider changing. Using a pencil, check your answers. If any of your answers are "no," read the corresponding information in this chapter for suggestions on how to make them a "yes." If the challenges are still too overwhelming, this is the time to consider moving to a more suitable living situation.

Checklist 4
RATE YOURSELF: EMOTIONAL ACTIVITY

Emotional Activity	Yes	No
Able to identify your emotional stress symptoms.		
Utilize good coping habits most of the time.		
Minimize poor coping habits.		
Have a viable financial and estate plan.		
Have Power of Attorney, Advanced Directives, and Last Will and Testament properly documented.		
Personal safety tips addressed.		
Be open to change and be willing to adapt.		

chapter 4

Keep Mentally Active

Are you afraid of losing your mental capacity as you age? Have you met older people who have lost their zest and meaning for life and you fear you may become like them? Are you worried you will no longer be appreciated in society? Do you wonder if you will become lethargic and lonely?

A common myth is that aging results in inevitable memory loss and a decrease in all cognitive abilities. Research does not support these claims. You may be surprised to hear the overwhelming majority of seniors retain their mental capacity with only mild cognitive decline. Certain areas of thinking remain completely stable. If you'd like to learn more about seniors' mental health, consult the Resource section at the end of this book or by researching online "healthy aging brain."

You have probably misplaced your phone or car keys on occasion. You might have forgotten the day of the week for a moment, or had days where the crossword puzzle was tougher to solve. These fleeting lapses of memory or reasoning should not cause concern. In the big picture, if these lapses do not affect your day-to-day activities, it is best not to worry about them.

Many factors beyond aging can affect our cognitive ability. Medications can cause mental dullness. Pain can affect our ability to concentrate or the speed of our actions. Hearing loss can affect our ability to process information. Our emotional state; whether we are hopeful or depressed, plays a significant role in our motivation to learn new things or apply sensible strategies to problem solving. Being aware of your physical and emotional state can help you gain insight regarding your true cognitive abilities.

As the head of your health-care team, you need to be able to communicate your health status to the professionals who will direct, provide advice, and care for you. A simple chart (see Diagram 3) to help you recognize typical age-related versus abnormal mental cognitive decline is included in this chapter. It's time to consult your doctor when the signs and symptoms of this decline begin to affect your day-to-day activities.

Keeping mentally active means challenging yourself in a variety of ways in order to build or strengthen neural connections in your brain. You may take your brain health for granted and not realize that it needs exercise just as the rest of your body does. As the saying goes, "If you don't use it, you lose it"! This applies to your brain as well as your body. Mental exercise doesn't have to be difficult or draining. As a matter of fact, it is proven to be more effective when you're enjoying the activity.

Mental exercises can range from simple to complicated activities. You'll make your brain work better by challenging yourself to learn in a variety of ways. We've included a list of suggestions (see section 2.1) to show you how to keep mentally active by becoming a life-long learner.

Healthy, mentally active seniors are the most capable to age safely in their homes. In fact, they thrive to stay alive! They are able to continually reinvent themselves as they deal with losses and find ways to live productively despite the changes associated with aging. They build strong social connections and find purpose in making a contribution to their own communities. This chapter explains several characteristics you can build on to find or keep your zest for life so you, too have the best chances of aging safely in your home.

Addressing each aspect of your being — body, mind, and spirit — is important when considering personal adaptations that will enable you to age safely in your home. Body, mind, and spirit are interconnected. While science has proven the connection between body and mind, the notion of spirituality is less tangible. Although it is important to the vast majority of us, our definition and expression of spirituality is broad-ranging and highly individual.

In many cultures, the elders of the community are respected for their wisdom and mature spirituality. The later years in life inspire many seniors to use their leisure time to contemplate and reflect on their past experiences. It is a time to ponder the meaning of life, beliefs, and what lies ahead. Some seniors use this time to summarize their experiences, values, life lessons, and precious memories. This time of reflection can provide an opportunity to share wisdom and leave a legacy to loved ones.

If you have a connection to a young person such as a grandchild, other relatives, or children of close friends, this can be an opportunity for mentorship. If you are so inclined, this mentorship can even be shared in a volunteer situation, creating bonds within your community.

In this chapter you are encouraged to address the mental and spiritual aspects of your being through nourishing your spirit and seeking joy and purpose in life.

1. Recognize Cognitive Changes

A normal part of aging involves some memory loss and decreased cognitive function. Diagram 3 is not a diagnostic tool, but it shows some differences between what is considered "normal" age-related cognitive decline and what is "abnormal" cognitive decline, which is an indicator to consult a health professional for further testing.

Recognizing your own mental cognitive state requires awareness and honesty. It is common for people to doubt or to be in denial about their fading memory, language skills, or judgment. Try to be objective and assess your mental health by referring to Diagram 3 as a general guideline. The sooner you identify the problem, the sooner it can be dealt with appropriately. Depending on the underlying cause, an early diagnosis and treatment could prevent your mental health condition from getting worse.

We may not always be able to recognize the signs of cognitive decline. Our brains will do their best to compensate for the changes. We will find new ways to help us remember names, directions, and information. We may participate less in discussions in order to hide our language difficulties. We may use more gestures to communicate simply, or say we

Diagram 3
COGNITIVE DECLINE

Age-Related Cognitive Decline	Abnormal Cognitive Decline
Occasionally forgetting appointments, some names, and phone numbers; yet able to remember them later.	Forgetting appointments, names of family members or close friends, phone numbers, and not being able to recall them later.
Able to function independently. Difficulty in holding attention when other distractions are happening at the same time.	Often unable to complete familiar and simple tasks or not understanding what numbers are, and how to make change.
Taking longer to find words or to get them out in conversation. The information is not lost completely, just harder to retrieve. Repeating stories on different occasions.	Frequent pauses and substitutions when finding words, making sentences difficult to understand. Repeating words or phrases during a conversation.
Occasionally forgetting street names or directions.	Getting lost in familiar surroundings and forgetting how you got there or why you ventured out.
Occasionally putting off seeing a doctor for what you think to be an insignificant condition.	Not able to recognize a medical problem that needs attention or wearing heavy clothing on a hot day.
Occasional mood changes.	Rapidly changing and varied mood swings.
Worrying about your memory but your family and close friends are not.	Your family and close friends are worrying about your memory, but you are not aware of any problems.

understand something when we don't. Some of these compensations in behavior may happen without us being aware of it. This is why it is important to remain open to what others have observed in your behavior. In most cases, your trusted loved ones will have your best interests at heart, so keep this in mind if you are feeling hurt or defensive. It is wise to listen to other's comments on your mental health then speak to your doctor for a medical opinion and proper diagnosis.

When you or a loved one believes you are exhibiting abnormal cognitive decline, do not jump to the conclusion that you have Alzheimer's disease, the most common form of a host of conditions that cause dementia. There can be many reasons for the changes you are experiencing, and some of them are reversible with treatment and rehabilitation. Conditions that can produce mental cognitive decline are depression, stroke, infection, head injury, vitamin and hormone deficiencies, medication incompatibility or over-medication, and alcohol-induced dementia. Your doctor will need to do a thorough assessment to determine the underlying causes of any significant mental cognitive decline.

The encouraging news is studies show that keeping your brain active can help reduce your risk of developing dementia, including Alzheimer's disease. This gives me hope on a personal level. Sadly, both of my parents had conditions that resulted in dementia. My mother died in 2002 from a rare form of Parkinson's. My father is living with Alzheimer's (and/or vascular dementia) after having mini-strokes and diabetes. Needless to say, my family history has inspired me to do whatever I can to optimize my future mental health and well-being! I know there is no absolute prevention for Alzheimer's disease; however, I also know there is ever-increasing research and data that shows many chronic conditions and diseases can be prevented by maintaining an active brain and a healthy lifestyle. I find this very empowering to know I am doing all I can to minimize the risk factors. Brain health is important! I have committed to doing mental exercises which are as important to me as my physical health regime.

2. Exercise Your Brain

Many of us are aware that we need to exercise our muscles in order to keep fit. When we don't exercise, it can become obvious that we are neglecting ourselves. Our body can become weak, tired, overweight, and/or sluggish. Our balance and coordination can become a challenge. We just don't feel strong and healthy. These signs and symptoms may be a reminder that we need to get more exercise.

What happens when we do not exercise our brains? The signs and symptoms of an unhealthy mental state may not be as obvious as when we don't exercise our bodies. We may not be aware that loneliness, boredom, lack of interest in activities or people, slower response time, and feeling stressed can all be indicators that we need to be more mentally fit.

2.1 Tips to keep mentally fit

The idea of having to keep mentally fit by challenging your brain may be a strange idea to some people. Don't worry, you won't have to train hard to become a champion chess player in order to succeed. Challenging your brain doesn't have to be difficult. It is actually most effective when you engage in something you enjoy. It can be as simple as picking up an object with your less dominant hand or as complex as learning to play a new musical instrument. The goal is to become a life-long learner by giving your brain a new experience and a workout every day.

Being a life-long learner will keep you mentally fit, more resilient, more engaged in your social life, and less stressed. There are many ways to achieve this; here are a few suggestions:

- ✓ Improve your concentration by focusing on one task at a time.
- ✓ Play memory or number games, solve puzzles, and engage in strategic games such as chess.
- ✓ Use your imagination when you read by trying to hear the different voices and tones in the dialogue. Visualize the detailed surroundings in the context.
- ✓ Go to a movie or an art gallery with a friend and discuss it afterwards.
- ✓ Break away from your routine by trying different foods or changing your walking route.
- ✓ Take up a new hobby such as music, travel, woodwork, or painting.
- ✓ Learn new ways to use the computer by taking online tutorials.
- ✓ Tune in to your senses by closing your eyes for a moment (while seated comfortably) and describe something that you have chosen to smell, taste, or touch.

Engaging in fun, new experiences qualifies as mental exercise. You may have seen or heard of the movie entitled *The Bucket List*. It was a huge box office success that told the story of two men crossing off their to-do wish list before "kicking the bucket"! If you're looking for ideas to engage your brain, spend some time thinking about what you'd really like to do that you've never done before. Return to the dreams and aspirations you had in your youth that you let pass by as you aged. It has been said that you don't die regretting the things you did, you die regretting the things you didn't do.

Don't let age become an excuse to stop following your passions. Choose the activities and interests that are still accessible to you. It can be a simple activity such as listening to rain pounding on a tin roof or concentrating on the lyrics in a song. It can be a complex event such as organizing a bridge tournament or taking a holiday to witness the wildebeest migration in the Serengeti. Checking items off your bucket list can give you a sense of achievement that will boost your vitality while exercising your brain.

Finding creative ways to adapt to your favorite pastimes is an excellent way to stimulate your brain. If you once loved to dance but now your arthritic knees are bothered by weight-bearing, try taking an aqua fit class. The buoyancy of the water will reduce the stress on your joints, and you'll get to enjoy the music in a different way. If you once cycled long distances and are feeling less steady, or don't want to venture as far, try exercising on a stationary bike that has virtual courses built into the monitor to provide a sense of traveling. Consider coaching or taking a supportive role in your favorite sporting events or hobbies. There are many ways to stay involved in the pastimes that you've always loved.

Take a moment now to write down the following:

- ✓ What activities brought you the most enjoyment in the past?
- ✓ What activities are you capable of now that might provide the same kind of satisfaction?

3. Have a Zest for Life

This statement might sound like a cliché or seem like a ridiculous challenge to some seniors. The key to achieving the zest for life is to continually discover, or rediscover, what is important to you. What you feel is important helps define your passions and these will enable you to establish goals and take action to maintain a value-added lifestyle. Seniors who continue to set reasonable goals, participate in activities, and interact socially have a higher quality of life and tend to live longer. These are the seniors who live life to the fullest.

As a senior, you have the ability to thrive on life's challenges regardless of your age or circumstances. Our challenge to you is to follow the personal and housing adaptations we've suggested for aging safely in your home. You'll cover the basics on how to achieve your optimal personal health and wellness and create a sustainable and healthy environment for yourself. Beyond these basics, you can also become a senior that has a zest for life.

If you were born between 1946 and 1964 you may be familiar with the term "Boomer Zoomer." We are the trendsetters of the Boomer generation. The term Zoomer reflects an attitude of living life to the fullest by engaging in life in an active manner. The Boomer Zoomers are now the pioneers of anti-ageism that are busting stereotypes and myths about getting older. We are redefining senior's roles and reinventing retirement. If you wish to boost your zest for life, research the Zoomer group and join their example of living life to the fullest.

3.1 Tips to create the zest for life

Attitude is the key. Seniors who have a positive outlook on life are also resilient, courageous, and grateful. They have positive self-esteem and, therefore, they believe they have something to offer to their loved ones and society. They are passionate about life and have many reasons to thrive.

There are many ways to develop a winning attitude. A winning attitude begins with fostering a sense of gratitude. Review the memories that bring you joy. Your perspective based on your life experience can make daily life become all the more precious. Acknowledge which aspects of life you are grateful for in the present. Focus on the abilities you still possess and make use of them.

Strengthen your resiliency by acknowledging what obstacles you have already overcome. Reward yourself for what you have been able to achieve despite the significant challenges you have been faced with. Recognize your ability to bounce back and tap into that source of strength when further challenges arise.

Get involved in activities that take courage and ambition. You may not be able to climb Mount Everest but you can take a gondola to view a scenic panorama somewhere you'd like to visit. Challenge ageist messages in the media by asserting yourself and demonstrating your value in society. Learn to identify and filter messages that do not promote your self-worth. Compete in friendly games to improve yourself, not to beat someone else.

Boost your self-esteem by taking the time for personal care and to dress in a way that makes you feel good about yourself. A popular motivational tool is to "Dress for Success"! As you get older your definition of success may change, but this advice still applies. As an active senior, you are likely still working, volunteering, or involved in social activities. Dress in a way that reflects an image of someone who cares about himself or herself. Spend time around people who genuinely appreciate you and make you feel alive and wanted.

Be passionate about life. This requires that you discover what motivates you and that you pursue your own desires. One passion that is often overlooked as we age is our sexuality. A winning attitude will help you overcome the sexual issues that can affect people older than the age of 50. Sex has the power to improve your physical and mental health, enhance relationships, and increase your lifespan. The need for intimacy is ageless, and it is possible to have an ongoing fulfilling sex life if this is one of your passions.

4. Make Time for Spiritual Practice

Each one of us has a unique way of experiencing spiritual purpose and joy. We place different values on our personal connection to our inner selves, our society, our environment, and our ancestors. We search for the meaning of life and death through different means; and we have different ways of meeting our spiritual needs.

At this stage of life, seniors have already had their families, have been productive in society, or have had other achievements and milestones that mark the passing of time. The reality and inevitability of the end of life becomes a very relevant focus for seniors. This focus brings to light the mystery of the afterlife and one's beliefs about spirituality.

4.1 Nourish your spirit

Taking time to nourish your spirit is a worthwhile endeavor that can add purpose and meaning to your everyday life. Some people find their spiritual practice provides clarity and enhances their ability to be at peace with themselves and others. Some people feel uplifted and joyful, creating a sense of optimism and a release of stress. Others feel more grounded in the present; able to concentrate, and act with kindness and compassion rather than reacting impulsively to life's challenges. Some people feel strengthened by belonging to a spiritual community, while others find comfort by drawing deeper into themselves or by connecting to nature.

People nourish their spirit in a variety of ways. Do what works for you. Many seniors are already aware of how and where they like to express their spirituality, but over time there may be barriers to accessing a place of worship. This can lead not only to spiritual loss, but also to social isolation and mental decline. If you are currently part of a religious community, use the resources it offers to assist you in getting to services or maintaining regular spiritual practice. Regardless of how you express your spirituality, ensure that you are able to get to the activities or places that are "good for your soul." Ask for the help you require.

If you have not developed a spiritual dimension and are interested in the benefits a spiritual practice can provide, consult with your innermost circle. They may help you define what brings you joy and purpose. Spirituality is a popular topic these days, and there is much literature online or in your local library or bookstore. Look at the titles that interest you and discuss the material with others to find what appeals to you and how you can access groups with similar philosophies.

To promote your own sense of purpose you may consider volunteering. Giving back does more than simply help others. It can build your self-esteem by putting years of your unique experience to practice. Choose a volunteer opportunity that will be fun and meaningful to you. Many organizations are happy to accommodate your time availability and energy level. Take the time to find the right fit for your interests and passions. Volunteering can build your self-esteem, make you feel valued in society, and improve your own health and wellness.

5. Rate Yourself: Mental and Spiritual Activities

Checklist 5 will help you evaluate whether or not you meet the criteria for obtaining your optimal mental and spiritual health and independence to age safely in your home. Apply the information to your current habits, not what you might consider changing. Using a pencil, check your answers. If any of your answers are "no," read the corresponding information in this chapter for suggestions on how to make them a "yes." If the challenges are still too overwhelming, this is the time to consider moving to a more suitable living situation.

Checklist 5
RATE YOURSELF: MENTAL AND SPIRITUAL ACTIVITY

Mental and Spiritual Activities	Yes	No
Able to recognize signs of cognitive decline.		
Understand there are many reasons for cognitive decline.		
Willing to speak to your health-care team and/or family members about your mental health.		
Actively improving your brain health with new activities.		
Willing to learn something new.		
Have a meaningful purpose in life.		
Do something that feeds your spirit.		
Volunteer or give back to your community in some way.		

part 2

Housing Aspect of Aging
Safely in Your Home

chapter 5

Rate Your Home

Where is my home located? Why do I want to stay here? What changes are needed to stay here safely? When do I need to change things? How can I make the necessary changes? Who can help? If you want to age safely in your home, write down your answers to these fundamental questions. This is the starting point for the housing aspect. Assessment can begin at any point in time. As you continue to age, rating your home should be an ongoing procedure.

Diagram 4: The Rate-Change Cycle can be a helpful visual aid regarding how to think through the process of making the necessary changes. Remember to keep the cycle going regularly to age safely in your home; rate your home often!

The knowledge and understanding gained from rating your home is a prime factor in paving the way for aging safely in your home. It is very important to get a clear and accurate assessment at the starting point. Don't tell yourself the little white lie about everything being OK.

Diagram 4
THE RATE-CHANGE CYCLE

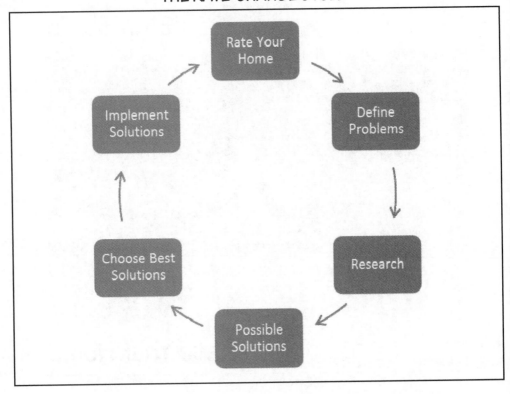

Things can probably be better! Be honest and realistic with regards to both the human aspect discussed previously in Part 1 and the housing aspect. Rating your home is best done in written form so you have a permanent record to revisit and update from time to time.

As a high school teacher, I know that assessing a student's starting point is a key requirement to help him or her move forward with his or her education. Written records are very important in setting goals, charting progress, and assessing setbacks. Ultimately, these written records are documents that highlight areas needing attention. For example, there's no point giving Johnny a plan to build a birdhouse if he doesn't know how to read technical drawings. Similarly, there's no point living in a three-level house, accessible only by stairs, if the person has arthritic knees that make climbing stairs difficult and painful.

Each of us has different needs that would make our home safer as we age and those needs change as the years go by. Many people have an innate sense of changes that would make their living situation more comfortable and safer. However, sometimes you need an independent observer to assess things more accurately. The best assessments are done by both you and an adviser.

Personally, as a 50-something-year-old man, I already know some changes that are necessary in my own home. For example, my morning shower still takes place on the slippery wet porcelain of my bathtub. My balance probably isn't quite as good as it once was despite still viewing myself as athletic and fit. Looking at my situation honestly, it might be time for me to get a nonskid shower mat. Will buying a mat only happen as a response to a fall? I hope not. Frankly, a nonskid shower mat is a change I need right now to make my home safer. There might be other changes that are needed right now, too. For example, if an outside observer viewed the path I take to the bathroom for my 4:00 a.m. bathroom break, usually in the dark, that person might suggest I get a night-light and clear the travel route of the clothing hamper and other tripping hazards.

In a word, *now* is always a good time to make changes that will make aging in your home safer. Procrastination is an enemy of safety. As the rate-your-home cycle continues throughout your golden years, do things right away. Regarding my own bathtub scenario, I've had visions of buying my new nonskid mat with my arm in a sling. That would certainly be foolish because it would be so easy to go make that purchase right now!

"How can I make the necessary housing changes?" This question is a big one. Not everyone is a handyman or knows someone with the knowledge and skills to tweak a home for aging safely in place. This is where some physical effort combined with a thinking cap is required. The information age affords everyone access to enormous volumes of how-to books, videos, webinars, blogs, and the list goes on. With a little effort and help, you can make many of the necessary changes to age safely in place.

For the changes that might need a reputable contractor, there's plenty of information out there on how to select the right person or company for the job. This book will help with the basics but each person's situation is unique. The Rate Your Home checklist in section 2 will help you sort out what is needed; other sections such as Choosing a Contractor in Chapter 8 will help you to accomplish the necessary changes.

There are probably many people willing to help you age safely in your home. Family, friends, and even the high school kid down the street looking to make a bit of extra cash can help to get things done. There are many more places to access the help needed to age safely in your home. When you're at the "who can help?" stage, be bold about asking for what you need. Refer to Chapter 2, section 3, to help you feel more comfortable about asking for help.

1. Assessing Your Location

Presumably you're in a home and neighborhood where you feel comfortable and safe. Maybe you're close to friends and family. Maybe your transit needs are fulfilled by being close to bus routes. Whatever the case, the fundamental issue is: "Can I age safely here or do I need to move?" This is what rating your home is all about. The overwhelming majority of seniors prefer to remain at home but it's important to ensure that can be done comfortably and safely.

The thought of moving can be daunting, but it's something that must be considered with an open mind if you want to age in place. Although staying and moving are opposing ideas, have an open mind when considering aging in place. You might be better off living elsewhere.

Of course, our intention is to help you age safely where you are now. Most people can do it with some awareness and adjustments. But make no mistake, in order to age safely in your current home, you will require some basic housing, location, and situation needs met that you might discover aren't possible after assessing your current housing situation. The process of assessment is designed to have you living in a home and neighborhood that provides comfort, safety, and peace of mind.

"Why do I want to stay in my home?" This question may be a hard one to answer. Often, you want to remain where you are in life because you're afraid of the unknown. It's a valid reason, but it also might be a weak reason. Although change is not easy, everything changes and adaptation is a necessary part of life. Changing your home as you age is not easy but comfort and safety needs change as you age.

Choosing to age safely in your home should mean you've carefully thought about your options and your current housing situation is the best option. Healthy living situations start with clear thinking and sound reasoning in relation to your capabilities.

Procrastinating a move that needs to be made, having too much stuff to sort through, being nervous and afraid of change — these are not good reasons for wanting to stay in your current living situation. Having helpful neighbors, having the perfect one-level house, living two blocks away from a supportive daughter and grandkids — these are very good reasons for wanting to remain in place.

Whatever your reasons for wanting to stay in place, you should consider those reasons understanding that issues such as personal isolation, personal security, falls prevention, physical inactivity, dietary needs, medical accessibility and, for some, cost factors should be the major focal points of reasoning because these are some important things to consider.

2. Rating Your Home

Let's begin with Checklist 6, which will help you evaluate whether or not your home meets the criteria for optimal home safety. Using a pencil, check your answers. Analyze your situation honestly and assess if you are finding any difficulties with these tasks; put a checkmark in either the "yes" or "no" column. **Note:** It is not necessary to do the tasks yourself but you must have a consistent, sustainable means for completing the tasks. For example, you might hire a gardener, housekeeper, or regular handyman whom you pay to complete certain tasks. The important issue is that the tasks are getting done consistently.

Any item that landed in the "yes" column of the checklist is more or less under control. Anything that landed in the "no" column needs some consideration and scrutiny. Take a close look at the No column items in relation to Diagram 4. You need to come up with solutions to these. For all those No items, you'll need to do the following:

✓ Identify the problems.

✓ Do some research regarding the solutions.

✓ Generate possible solutions based on your research and cost factors.

✓ Decide what would be your best solutions.

✓ Reassess the practicality of staying in place, knowing that any No items that can't be moved to the Yes column make staying safe in your home more difficult.

The end goal of rating your home is to identify items that can be adapted or improved to make day-to-day life easier and safer. If most items on the checklist are under control, staying safely in your home will also be under control. If too many checklist items are in the No column

Checklist 6
RATE YOUR HOME

Activity	Yes	No
Maintenance		
Yard work: Able to take care of the yard.		
Housekeeping: Able to keep the house clean and tidy.		
Outdoor (house): Able to repair and maintain exterior of the house.		
Indoor (house): Able to repair and maintain interior of the house.		
Seasonal issues: Able to take care of seasonal issues such as shoveling snow, raking leaves, and/or installing Christmas lights.		
Outdoor Living		
Walkways and surfaces: Able to clean and safely walk on walkways and surfaces.		
Elevation changes: Able to walk safely across steps, slopes, and uneven terrain.		
Furniture: Able to safely use and walk around outdoor furniture.		
Weather protection: Outdoor living areas and entrances are protected from sun, wind, rain, snow, and ice.		
Lighting: Outdoor areas are well lit.		
Indoor Living		
Doorways: Easy to walk through with no tripping hazards and sufficiently wide for assistance devices such as walkers or wheelchairs. Door handles and locks are easy to use.		
Windows: Clearly marked if difficult to see and easy to open and close.		
Hallways: Easy to use with no tripping hazards.		
Flooring: Level, even, and secure with no tripping hazards.		
Closets and storage: Easy and convenient to use with sufficient space to avoid clutter in living zones and travel routes.		
Traffic flow: Main travel routes are clear, uncluttered, and if necessary, provide sufficient handrails.		
Bedroom: Easy to use. No tripping hazards.		
Bathroom: Easy to use. No slipping or tripping hazards. Toilet and washing facilities are appropriate for occupant's strength and balance.		
Kitchen: Easy to use. No tripping hazards. Minimum fire hazard and fire protection equipment in place.		
Stairs: Easy to use. No tripping hazards. Adequate handrails.		
Furnishings: Easy to use and don't interfere with main travel routes.		
Lighting: Adequate lighting throughout house but especially at danger zones such as stairs, entrances, bathrooms, kitchens, and main bedroom.		
Heating: Adequate heating and cooling systems throughout house that provide comfort even in unusual seasonal temperature/humidity fluctuations.		

Detection systems: Security, smoke, carbon monoxide, and motion-detector lighting is adequate and monitored regularly.		
Fall Prevention		
Tripping hazards: Minimal tripping hazards such as clutter, throw rugs, uneven flooring, poor lighting, and narrow travel routes.		
Slipping hazards: Minimal slipping hazards such as flooring areas that get wet, slippery floors, or inadequate grab bars.		
Furnishing hazards: Easy-to-use, stable furniture that doesn't infringe on travel routes.		
Stairs: Easy-to-use stairs with adequate handrails and lighting, consistent risers (steps), and uncluttered steps and landings.		
Flooring: Even, consistent, secure nonslip flooring with no loose tripping hazards.		
Inside and outside: Adequate railings and grab bars throughout house especially in the bathroom and bedroom.		
Other		
Location: Suitable location for accessing amenities.		
Transport: Able to get places outside the home easily.		
Costs: Maintenance and repair costs are manageable and sustainable.		

and can't be adapted or changed, then aging safely in your home is not a practical option.

Remember the goal is to age safely, and if you need to relocate to age safely in your home, now is the time to plan for it. After completing Checklist 6, you will need to make some hard choices regarding the number of items you can handle in your current housing situation.

3. Getting the Work Done

When you have determined all the necessary safety changes to your home can be achieved and they are realistic, it's worth considering the practical aspects of getting work done before the work actually begins. Sometimes getting work done is easy but on other occasions it can take considerable time, expense, and effort. Before you get the work done, take time to research, think, and plan.

Based on Checklist 6, you will have identified some areas of concern. Some needs are more important than others. Do more than think about getting those items addressed. Research who can do the work, what will it cost, and how much time will it take. Consider whether getting the work done will allow you to age safely in place in the long term, or if it is a temporary solution. Is it acceptable to you to be disrupted by a six-month major renovation or would you rather not go through that hassle? Do you want to spend $10,000 on replacing slippery hardwood floors or would you rather take that dream vacation to Bermuda?

If the list of items to be done is short, you're probably already aging safely in your home with the ability and means to take care of issues as they arise. However, if the list is long, planning how to accomplish everything in a smooth coordinated manner is important and will certainly be time well spent.

The next four chapters contain tips and suggestions for getting work done. As a former draftsman, estimator, and project manager in both residential and commercial construction, I should forewarn you: getting work done can be a frustrating experience if planning and organization are not something you do well. It's called work for a reason! Start by prioritizing. Organize any items that can be grouped together. For example, if there are electrical issues that need fixing, one work order and one bill will be much more economical and convenient. If finances are an issue, separate items into inexpensive and expensive. Separate items into technically specialized and nontechnical. Regardless of how you group work items, the important issue is to spend some time planning and organizing. It's the only way to get things done efficiently and economically.

Worksheet 1 will help you organize the work that needs to be done. You can print the form using the download kit link at the end of this book. You can also complete the form on your computer by using the MS Word program. You may choose to organize this worksheet differently but it is very important to get organized before the work begins. Make sure you get several quotes for each work item.

4. Cost Factors

Aging safely in your home has cost factors. With regard to housing, sometimes cost boils down to how much you are able to take care of without paying for outside help. It's much less expensive if you do things yourself rather than hire someone to do them. The person who is a handyman, has a handyman son or daughter, or has a helpful neighbor is at a definite advantage to the person who needs to outsource everything.

Caution: It's important to get things done right. For example, saving a few dollars having a grab bar installed by the high school student who lives down the road is only beneficial if he or she knows the grab bar needs to be screwed into studs rather than just mounted on the drywall. Poor workmanship creates its own hazards. There's always a need to balance costs and proper workmanship.

There are many ways to keep costs under control. There are sometimes government grants and incentives for seniors. Check with your local seniors' center, seniors' organization, and/or government office to see if there are grants for your situation.

Sometimes you can source products at wholesale or contractor prices. Social media can be a resource for identifying economical and efficient companies or individuals. By sourcing products and labour efficiently, costs can be kept to a minimum.

The construction, renovation, and home adaptation industries have a wide-ranging level of costs and professionalism. Ultimately, it's always a case of buyer beware, so do your research when trying to balance quality workmanship and affordability. It's important to choose contractors wisely and systematically. Sometimes keeping costs under control is a by-product of choosing the right contractor. (Refer to Chapter 8 for more information about choosing a contractor.)

ORGANIZE THE WORK

Work Item	Company Name, Contact Person, and Phone Number	Cost Estimate	Notes
Specify exactly the work to be done.			*Record notes that are important such as availability and other information that helps you to decide who will do the work.*
Example: Install exterior motion light (Sunbeam Pro by Stargaze Manufacturing) centered above entrance door to garage.	YVo Electrical Company Joe Smith 555-555-5555	$455.00	Can't do the job until January. Highly recommended by Uncle Bob.
	GMo Handyman Services Jill Jones 555-444-4444	$375.00	Can start anytime. Old friend of Dad's. Good work but slow.
	Panorama Ridge Technologies Terry Doe 555-333-3333	$440.00	Can start anytime. Installed neighbor's motion lights. Quote is valid for 30 days.

chapter 6

Make Your Home Comfortable

Is your home still as comfortable for you as it once was? Is your home still providing you with a feeling of safety and security? Is your home helping or hindering your physical, social, emotional, mental, and spiritual needs? Are you happy in your home?

Your home should be comfortable. In Chapter 1, we noted that we all have physical, social, emotional, mental, and spiritual needs. Making your home comfortable means it is set up in a way that fulfills your needs.

An excellent example of a very suitable home for aging safely is a small one-level home owned by an 80-something relative. This home really hits the mark for comfort. It is set up and maintained very well making it a very good place to age safely and comfortably. The home is very easy and safe to walk around both inside and outside because it's level and flat with no stairs. It is small and compact. It has comfortable chairs and beds. The travel routes through the home and around the home are clear and uncluttered. It is warm in the winter yet cool in the summer. It is simply a very pleasant living space. Over the years, I have heard many visitors compliment the owner by expressing their feelings or observations: "I really love your home," or "Your home is so warm and inviting," or "Wow, it's so nice that you don't have to navigate stairs." People seem to enjoy being in this home which really invites social interaction to the life of the owner. For me, I find the home calm, serene, and harmonious. It often improves my mood and takes me to my own place of emotional, mental, and spiritual tranquility. This is a home that oozes comfort and really helps to take care of the owner's needs.

Human beings, for the most part, are social creatures who need to enjoy the company of each other to feel happy and secure. It follows that our home should be set up to encourage social interactions. When you set up your home, think about where you can gather with other people and set up areas to accommodate getting together with one or more people. If you enjoy outdoor living, create a comfortable gathering area on a patio or porch. If you enjoy playing cards, your kitchen table should be adaptable to accommodate a card game. If you enjoy one-on-one coffee sessions, make sure you have a great coffee maker and a suitable place to sit and chat. Obviously, each person has his or her own favorite way to socialize. Your home should be set up to accommodate those social interactions.

Setting up your home in an emotionally comforting manner is more difficult to define. Think in terms of creating feelings of happiness. For example, Yvonne and I feel very connected to nature, so on an emotional level, a home that echoes the natural world is wonderful for our peace of mind. We like the sound of running water. We like pictures, paintings, or photos of the great outdoors on our walls. We like house plants because they help freshen the air while bringing beauty into our home. Plants help to take care of us. We like aquariums because the water and slow movements of the fish have a calming effect. At other times in our lives, we've benefitted tremendously by having birds or dogs as part of the family and home environment. All of these noted items give us the best possible home environment for creating feelings of contentment and happiness.

Creating comfort for your mental and spiritual pursuits is very similar to the earlier noted physical, social, and emotional aspects. You first need to define what keeps you mentally and/or spiritually active and then you need to set up your home to accommodate those pursuits.

With regards to mental comfort, in my home, everyone enjoys reading as a mental activity so we have set up a comfortable reading place using my grandpa's favorite chair, which I inherited, and a reading lamp situated right beside the fireplace. It's such a great place to stimulate our minds in contented comfort.

Yvonne finds peace and tranquility in the spiritual practice of meditation. She has placed a Buddha statue outside our window which helps quiet her mind and creates a calming environment for meditation. Again, it's not important what you do, it's just important that you make some efforts to set up your home for consistently being able to go to a comfortable place to engage in your favorite mental and spiritual activities.

1. Basic Comforts

How do you make your home comfortable? Start by paying attention to your basic needs. When we speak of making your home comfortable we'd be well served to refer back to Chapter 1. Think in terms of securing physical, social, emotional, mental, and spiritual comfort. Also, think in terms of taking care of your five senses: sight, sound, touch, taste, and smell. If you go about setting up your home with the intent of satisfying these needs, you are likely to be successful in creating a very comfortable home environment.

Physically, create a temperate environment which is warm in the winter yet cool in the summer; create a physically helpful space which means it's easy for your body to get what it needs — nourishment, exercise and rest, to name a few. We need furniture that is ergonomically beneficial and comfortable. We all need a quiet and comfortable place to sleep, and our sensory system wants a pleasing environment. Think about what makes you physically comfortable and add those things to the list of requirements for your home.

1.1 Tips to make your home more comfortable

If you're not sure what might make your home physically comforting, scientifically speaking, you might be surprised to learn the following tips for making your home comfortable:

✓ Natural sunlight is better for you than artificial light because artificial light can make you sleepier and more stressed. During the day, open the window coverings and let the sun shine in! Skylights are also great for letting in the natural sunlight.

- ✓ Smells can affect your mood. For example, citrus stimulates, and lavender or vanilla helps you to relax. Use scents to make your home smell pleasant.

- ✓ Get some house plants. They improve the visual appearance of the home while helping to improve air quality.

- ✓ Start your day right. Begin by making your bed; studies have shown this simple task can improve productivity and happiness. After making your bed, have the most important meal of the day — breakfast.

- ✓ Turn on some mellow music. It can help lower heart rate, blood pressure, and stress levels.

- ✓ Set up your bedroom for sleep. Studies show blue walls are best for creating longer, more relaxing sleeps. Get rid of the ambient light from cell phones, televisions, and laptops because they interfere with sleep.

2. Organizing Your Home

Organizing your home is one of the best and least expensive things you can do to create comfort. It's also very important for aging safely in your home. Most people have an innate sense of what needs organizing; it often starts with de-cluttering. Did you know that if you haven't used something within the past year, it's very unlikely you'll need it or use it again? So why hold on to things you don't really need? You can truly benefit your body, mind, and soul by getting rid of unused and unwanted things; and the bonus is that others can benefit from receiving those items. Keep in mind that less clutter creates more space which can open up and widen travel routes; getting rid of clutter helps make the home safe with less stuff to maneuver around.

2.1 Tips for organizing your home

There are hundreds of ways to organize your home. It's not so important how you organize your home; it's important that you do it. There are several key areas to organize to age safely in your home:

- ✓ De-clutter walking routes, all living areas, and high-traffic areas.
- ✓ Create a suitable exercise zone.
- ✓ Design areas to encourage socializing.
- ✓ Create areas to exercise your mind (e.g., reading, games, or hobby zones).

- ✓ Decorate your home in a way that appeals to your emotions (e.g., art, photos, inspirational messages, artifacts from your travels).
- ✓ Clear travel routes such as hallways and keep them well lit.
- ✓ Ensure frequently used items are easily accessible.
- ✓ Create areas to engage your spiritual practice.
- ✓ Ensure infrequently used items are stored out of the way.
- ✓ Give away, sell, or discard unused items.
- ✓ Create a secure place to take care of your paperwork.

3. Wants versus Needs

When I look around my home, I ask myself, What do I *want*? The answer to that question is a new television. I could also ask myself, What do I *need*? The answer to that question is more extensive. I need a nonslip bath mat, more storage space, and a new light fixture globe in the living room. My needs are much more important than my wants but human nature being quite predictable, the TV (wants) will probably arrive before the other more important items (needs) despite being collectively less expensive to purchase.

When it comes to aging safely in your home, your human nature may be a barrier to overcome. Your needs are much more important than your wants and those needs must take precedence. Unfortunately, many seniors continue to place the wants ahead of needs because that's how they've done things in the past. To be frank, in the past you may have gotten away with placing your wants ahead of your needs. Moving forward, you'll discover you want less and need more.

I know some seniors who cringe at the thought of installing handrails around the walking routes of their yard or in a garden. The main reasons for this are either because they don't like the look of handrails or they do not want to admit they need to use them. However, if they are unsteady on their feet, handrails are necessary and the visual impact should be of limited concern.

I must admit it's a difficult shift in thinking because you can convince yourself that you'll be just fine without the handrails. As you age, preventive measures become increasingly important. If you're unsteady on your feet, you need something to help steady you regardless of the optics of that type of assistance. Getting what you need requires a significant shift in thinking. As you age, your needs might not be visually or aesthetically pleasing but you'll be living in a new reality where your needs are more urgent than your wants. To age safely in your home, it will be worth making changes, regardless of the optics of those changes.

The North American culture is youth oriented; we are bombarded daily with images based on youth, beauty, strength, and independence. It's a nice illusion but as we age many of us need hearing aids, walkers, canes, adult pads, and orthopedic shoes, all of which aren't particularly flattering with regards to beauty, strength, and independence. Part of aging safely in your home involves making wise adjustments to how you live and what's truly important. It becomes easier when you accept the mental shift to prioritize *needs* over *wants*.

4. Maintaining Your Home

Maintaining your home as you age can be a real challenge. As you become less comfortable with bending down or scrubbing floors or the many tasks that require a bit of elbow grease, you need to get creative and thoughtful about how to do these troublesome yet important tasks. Keep in mind that in order to age safely in your home, your home needs to be cleaned on a regular basis. You need to keep doing maintenance tasks, and if you can't do them, or have no one to do them for you, this is a problem that needs a suitable solution.

One good thing about maintaining your home as you age is the fact that the process is also a form of exercise. When we're younger, cleaning or maintaining a home is a chore but as we age it transforms into a form of physical fitness. This is a big bonus because if we think of it in this way, we're killing two birds with one stone.

Maintaining your home is something worth considering in a practical sense. Many tasks can be simplified or adapted to either make the task itself easier or to make the task easier on your body. Worksheet 2 offers suggestions for adapting and/or simplifying household tasks to make them easier.

4.1 Cost considerations

Comfort often has a price but you don't necessarily need to spend money to be comfortable. There are many things you can do that won't cost a dime that can greatly improve the comfort of your home.

I like to tell the story of witnessing a young Tanzanian mom carefully sweeping the ground around her mud hut. Yes, it was a mud hut

Worksheet 2
SIMPLIFY THE MAINTENANCE

Maintenance Activity	Simplify
Yard Work	
Outdoor	Pace yourself by giving yourself more time to do less work. Ensure you have the best ergonomic tools possible, including stable ladders and extendable washers and brushes.
Cutting grass	Use a self-propel lawn mower.
Weeding	Use a stand-up weeding tool.
Leaves removal	Use a leaf blower or light-weight rakes.
Snow removal	Use a snow blower or ergonomic shovel.
Power-washing	Use with a trigger-handle lock.
Housekeeping	
Indoor	Pace yourself by giving yourself more time to do less work. Ensure you have the best ergonomic tools possible.
Vacuuming	Pace yourself by vacuuming one room at a time. Ensure you have a comfortable, easy-to-use upright vacuum.
Washing floors	Use stand-up mops and sponges and smaller cleaning solution buckets (light weight).
Dusting	Use a long-handled duster.
Sweeping floors	Use a long-handled dust scoop.
Cleaning windows and mirrors	Use a long-handled squeegee.

and, yes, she was sweeping dirt on dirt but when she was finished everything looked so neat and tidy. She did this every day. It was very dignified and ultimately, very comforting. If money and costs are issues, focus on the many things you can do that won't cost money, such as de-cluttering, good housekeeping, and keeping linens washed and clean.

If money is not an issue, focus on things that will make day-to-day living easier and more comfortable by fixing any issues you might find difficult. If washing floors, cleaning windows, and cleaning washrooms have become increasingly difficult, perhaps it's time to get a housekeeper twice a month. If you can afford it, paying someone to help you is not cheating! Having the ability to spend money on things you want or need is why you worked all those years.

Most seniors at some point need someone to help with yard work and small fixes around the home. It's worth spending some time and energy to find someone who can help you with these types of tasks. Students, retired persons who are handy around the house, and community-minded individuals are all possible sources for help at a minimal cost.

5. Securing Your Home

Consider safety and security for a moment. As you age, safety and security becomes more important, generally speaking. We feel more vulnerable as we age; therefore, we want more safety and security measures in place. For comfort and peace of mind around these issues there are many things we can do.

5.1 Tips for securing your home

The following items are basic checks to ensure your safety and security issues are under control:

- ✓ Ensure door locks and deadbolts or security chains are in place.
- ✓ Ensure primary and secondary window locks are in place.
- ✓ Consider installing window grates or bars.
- ✓ Make sure your security alarm is functioning properly with a charged backup battery. If you don't have a security alarm, consider installing a monitored alarm.
- ✓ Prepare an emergency security plan with a reliable, able-bodied neighbor.
- ✓ Install a peephole in entry doors, if you don't already have one, and use it to identify people knocking at your door.
- ✓ Get a cell phone and always carry it with you.
- ✓ Ensure there is adequate lighting around your home.
- ✓ Trim bushes and store ladders properly.

chapter 7

Adapt Your Home

Are you discovering changes in your physical capabilities as you age? Do you wonder about how you can adapt your home to make your life easier, safer, and more comfortable? Do you wonder how you can make necessary changes to your home while keeping costs and expenses down?

I recently removed a set of bifold doors from a laundry closet. The 80-year-old owner simply didn't want the added step of opening a set of doors when she had to do laundry. The doors also stuck out into the hallway and interfered with walking space when opened. They were purely cosmetic rather than important functional doors. This minor adaptation of removing the laundry closet doors makes the process of doing laundry simpler for the owner who is aging safely and smartly in her home. I think she is always on the lookout for any little tweak that will make her life easier. I probably don't need to tell you that a bunch of "little bit simpler" adds up to a whole lot simpler! It's really worthwhile to look around your house to discover adaptations that will make your life simpler, more convenient, and safer.

The term "adapt" (according to *Webster's New World Dictionary*) means "to make suitable, esp. by changing" or "to adjust (oneself) to new circumstances." According to this definition, adaptations are especially pertinent for seniors. They are learning to live in new circumstances as the aging process brings new realities to their lives. These new realities require that they make ongoing changes and adjustments for living in their ever-changing circumstances. Ultimately, people wanting to age safely in their home should want to make things more suitable for their changing needs.

We have already discussed the fact that aging safely in your home involves both personal and home adaptations. There's not a clean separation where one ends and the other begins but hopefully you'll recognize the interwoven nature of personal and home adaptations. For the purposes of this book, we will also define adaptations as the minor tweaks that are helpful or required to age in place. Chapter 8 will cover the major structural changes and more costly items that might be required to age safely in your home.

The following suggestions are adaptive changes that have enabled others to age safely in their homes or at least simplified the reality of aging in place. We are not implying this is a complete list but it will certainly point out some areas to consider in regards to adapting your home as you age.

1. Yard/Outdoor Space

Adapting your outdoor living/yard space can be very beneficial for aging in place. If set up well, your outdoor living space has the potential to provide exercise, sunshine, food, and storage. You can connect with nature, pursue hobbies, maintain vehicles, and socialize with family, neighbors, and friends. There are so many benefits to adapting your outdoor space to help you as you age.

One of the most important aspects of adapting outdoor/yard space is to think in terms of fall prevention. Uneven, slippery, or poorly lit areas need to be adapted for easier and safer movement around yards and outdoor areas. The following home adaptations may help improve your outdoor living zones:

✓ Spend some time thinking about how you would like to use your outdoor living/yard space. Planning and designing how to use your yard in more practical and useful ways is time very well spent. The resultant changes and adaptations can lead to miraculous transformations. Don't hesitate to include other knowledgeable people in your circles during the design process. Think in terms of practical, functional, low maintenance, and safe.

✓ Trim vegetation and remove troublesome trees, bushes, and roots.

✓ Add motion lights in the front and back of your home.

✓ Create consistent grades or ramps to eliminate stairs or inconsistent elevation changes. As we age, inconsistencies underfoot can be tripping hazards. We can sometimes eliminate these inconsistencies simply by pushing a bit of dirt around. Of course, sometimes there's more work involved which brings us to the world of renovations (see Chapter 8).

✓ Eliminate steps and/or irregular shaped steps and inconsistent risers. Many step inconsistencies are found outside in garden areas. I have been on many garden steps that are difficult to navigate because of irregularities and sometimes there's a quick fix if you're willing to do a bit of grunt work with a shovel or mortar/concrete. Don't hesitate to call in the professionals to correct stair inconsistencies because these situations can be serious tripping/falling zones.

2. Entryways

Adapting entryways will make your entry to and exit from the home simpler and safer. Entryways are important zones for home safety. There are many things that can be done to create more user-friendly entryways:

✓ Get a welcome sign, door chimes, or hanging basket to create a warm, welcoming atmosphere.

✓ Install a peephole if you don't already have one. A peephole is one of the simplest and least expensive security measures that you can install. It allows you to see who's at your front or back door without opening it.

✓ Consider keyless entry and security bolts. A keyless entry requires that you're able to remember the entry code that needs to be punched in to lock or unlock the door. If you have memory issues, this might not be a good adaptation.

✓ Amplify doorbells or ringers. In cases of extreme hearing loss, you can also connect your doorbell to a bright flashing light that will get your attention when you can't hear well. Depending on how handy you or those in your circle are with electrical issues, this sort of adaptation might drift into the renovation zone rather than adaptations.

✓ Consider self-closers. Self-closers are spring-loaded mechanisms that close the door for you. This can be a blessing or a curse depending on the individual. Self-closers are responsible for locking many people out of their homes, so think about whether this type of adaptation will help you or hurt you before installing these simple devices.

✓ Get some contrasting paint or finishes on door thresholds. Eliminating tripping hazards is very important as you age. Doors often have a slightly raised portion called a threshold that can sometimes trip people if it's not noticed and stepped over. Applying some contrasting paint or finish often makes a threshold more visible and obvious. The contrasting color can also help with depth perception.

✓ Create space for shoe storage and coats that de-clutters the entryway. If your home is without a closet, or even has an overflowing closet, install some hooks to hang coats and create some space to store shoes. Shoe storage can be as simple as a cardboard box. The important issue for this adaptation is that tripping hazards and clutter are eliminated.

✓ Place a chair near entryways so you can sit down while putting on or taking off your shoes.

3. Doors and Windows

Doors can be troublesome as we age, for several reasons. Doors require a certain level of hand and foot dexterity as we need to hold and often activate the handle as well as traverse across a threshold of some sort. Doors also require a certain amount of space for swinging. As we all know some doors are more troublesome to operate than others.

When it comes to adapting doors for aging safely in your home, there are many things that can be done. The following suggestions can help you adapt your doors to make them less bothersome:

- ✓ Sand or plane sticky or binding doors. If you remove a sticky door from its hinges by pulling the hinge pins, the part that is binding or rubbing will usually be quite obvious because the binding or rubbing portion will be wearing differently than the rest of the door. To eliminate this, you simply need to remove some material at the identified area by sanding or planing. It should be noted that sometimes a door is not hanging properly or has been damaged. Over time, doors can get loosened hinges or sag or sometimes door frames can change shape due to the house settling over time.

- ✓ Replace doorknobs with lever-style handles. These types of handles are much easier to use because they don't require gripping pressure; one simply needs to push down on the handle.

- ✓ Remove unnecessary doors. The example at the beginning of this chapter described a situation where removing a door was in the best interest of convenience and safety. Not all doors need to be there, and not all doors are useful.

- ✓ Do some maintenance work on your doors. (e.g., lubricate, tighten hinges and hardware, replace door stops and closers, if required).

- ✓ Highlight thresholds by using contrasting paints or finishes.

- ✓ Redo weather stripping on exterior doors, if required. Weather stripping is usually made from some sort of rubber or foam. It helps to seal the door thereby keeping out cold or hot air depending on the season. Unfortunately, weather stripping wears down or becomes damaged over time. It sometimes needs replacing.

Windows can also be troublesome as we age for several reasons. Windows can become corroded and sticky, they can be zones for heat loss and drafts, and they can create security risks. In the case of sliding patio doors, which are effectively a door and window all-in-one, they can be hazards for walking into. Some suggestions for adapting the windows, including patio doors, are as follows:

- ✓ Place suction-cup ornaments on patio doors to bring attention to the fact that there's a window there.

- ✓ Re-caulk windows to reduce heat loss or drafts. Caulking is filler. It is used in construction to fill small gaps between materials that aren't fitting perfectly. Caulking is used most commonly around windows and doors. These are places that dissimilar materials come together and seldom fit perfectly. Modern houses are sealed around doors and windows using various kinds of construction caulking. For best adhesion, you should remove old caulking and thoroughly clean and dry areas to be re-caulked and then follow the manufacturer's recommendations regarding conditions and temperatures for re-caulking.

✓ Do some maintenance work on your windows (e.g., lubricate cranks and opening devices, clean sliding window tracks, repair or replace window coverings).

✓ Ensure window locks are in good working order and get some secondary security measures such as secondary adjustable window stops or track wood stops.

4. Hallways

Hallways are simple traffic zones that really only serve the purpose of getting you from one place to another. There's not much to be adapted in a hallway, but the following suggestions might help to make them more user friendly:

✓ Install more and/or better lighting with a three-way switch to control lights both as you enter the hallway and as you exit the hallway. A three-way switch is an electrical term that refers to a light or switches that can be controlled (turned on or off), from two separate locations. Although I've mentioned it here, it's more accurately a renovation unless you have electrical expertise.

✓ Install night-lights. Night-lights come in a variety of styles and can be activated in many ways. They can be physically turned on and off. They can be light activated, whereby they come on automatically in darkness. They can be on timers, whereby you set the on and off time. They also can be motion activated, whereby they turn on whenever they detect movement.

✓ Install smoke and carbon monoxide detectors. Every household should have a properly functioning smoke and carbon monoxide detector but it's especially important for seniors who don't move quite as quickly as they used to and whose senses have dulled over the years. It's also important to check these devices periodically to ensure they continue to operate properly. Remember to change the battery every year by making it a spring or fall task that is done when the time change occurs. This way it is easy to get in the habit of doing this yearly.

✓ Install or repair handrails.

✓ Place a chair at the ends of long hallways or at stair landings if there's sufficient room for safely placing a "resting" chair.

5. Closets and Storage

Although closets and storage spaces don't provide much opportunity for adaptations, these areas allow you the opportunity to de-clutter, which is a very important aspect of aging safely in your home. Adapting these areas to allow for easier access as well as rearranging for creating more space are probably the main considerations for these areas. Closest and storage space might feel like wasted space sometimes but it's very useful if you want to live in an organized, tidy, and safe manner. Try some of these suggestions regarding storage areas and closets:

✓ Remove doors.

✓ Install shelving.

✓ Install hooks and create areas to hang items.

✓ Add lighting or provide a hook for mobile lighting. Not all storage areas and closets have lighting. It can be helpful to install hooks in unlit storage areas and get a portable light that can be moved from place to place.

6. Living/Family Rooms

Living or family rooms are the hub of any home. In combination with the kitchen, these are the areas where many people will spend most of their indoor waking hours. It's worth your while to be constantly on the lookout for adaptations that will make your life easier. There are so many adaptations available. Consider some of the following to help you be more comfortable and safe in your living/family room:

✓ Remove throw rugs because they are tripping hazards.

✓ Rearrange furniture for easier travel routes.

✓ Secure power bars at easy-to-reach locations. Bending down to plug in electrical items can be a hassle but worse than that it can throw you off balance, too. Don't be limited by the location of wall outlets. You can adapt those wall outlets to more convenient locations by using power bars. You can also secure power bars at more convenient heights by using a variety of mounting devices such as pipe clamps, metal strapping, or angle iron/aluminum. Cords are tripping hazards so having them securely tucked out of the way is very important. Many seniors just don't see cords on the ground, so it's important to keep them away from travel routes. Tucking them under carpets or attaching them to the wall are some suggestions.

✓ Consider getting remote control electrical controllers. These are convenient remote control electrical devices. They can make turning on and off items such as lamps, Christmas tree lights, and night-lights more convenient and safer. Some of these devices are controlled by handheld controllers, some are controlled by sound, such as clapping, or motion activated. These devices can be an excellent safety feature if you fear being thrown off balance by reaching or bending down to plug in electrical devices.

✓ Add risers to furniture to make standing up from chairs easier. A riser as the term relates to furniture is anything that adds height to a chair, seat, stool, or couch. One can create a raised base, build or buy raised castors or floor protectors, or even change short legs to tall legs. Adding risers to furniture does take a little creativity and ingenuity but the end goal is to create heightened, stable seating that is easier to stand up from.

✓ De-clutter.

✓ Get some portable heaters and coolers or fans. Keeping your living environment at the right temperature is sometimes difficult depending on the size of your home and fluctuations in outdoor temperatures. Some locations have the possibility of radical temperature changes within a given day. It's often beneficial to have a portable heater, fan, or air-conditioner to assist you in regulating the temperature in your home. Dehumidifiers can also be useful under certain weather conditions.

✓ Add more lighting.

7. Kitchen

The kitchen is probably the most consistently used area of any home. The number of possibilities for adapting the kitchen is endless. What adaptations are best for you really depends on how you use your kitchen and your own physical challenges. Whether you're a gourmet chef or a TV-dinner type, take some time to consider some of the following adaptations to your kitchen:

✓ Rearrange dishes and cookware for easier access. Arranging your kitchen utensils, dishes, glasses, and food in the most convenient and accessible manner is important and it changes over time.

Think about the items in your kitchen that are used most frequently. Those items should be front and center in the most accessible and convenient locations. Bending down excessively, overreaching, and having to use a stool to access high locations are things that should be minimized. A good rule of thumb is to think, plan, and set up your kitchen for your current dietary and cooking habits.

✓ Remove throw rugs because these are tripping hazards.

✓ Purchase some age-friendly utensils and appliances. There are so many helpful utensils and appliances that we could probably write a separate book to cover all the possibilities. There are devices to help you open a jar, electrical can openers, built-in ice and water dispensers on many refrigerators, battery powered cork removers for wine bottles, and the list goes on and on. You need to note the problems you're having in the kitchen as they arise and then investigate the many products that can help you to solve the problem.

✓ Replace cabinet hardware with easy-to-grip handles if the ones you have are now difficult to use.

✓ Replace or remove mechanical or magnetic cabinet clasps if they are troublesome.

✓ Turn down the hot water heater to a safe level (about 120 degrees Fahrenheit or 49 degrees Celsius).

✓ Consider getting more freezer space. Obviously, extra freezer space doesn't need to be in the kitchen. It could be in a garage, laundry room, or well-ventilated closet/storage space. Extra freezer space allows you to make extra meals when you have the inspiration to cook. Premade meals are a dietary adaptation that many seniors find helpful and convenient.

✓ Get a fire extinguisher installed in a handy location in this room.

✓ Consider getting a stove monitor that will turn off the stove if someone hasn't been in the kitchen for 5, 10, or 15 minutes. This is a good safety device for individuals prone to memory lapses.

8. Bedroom

Bedrooms are a zone where we are not necessarily alert and focused. We are often either sleepy or just waking up. With regards to some adaptive measures that you could consider for bedrooms, we offer the following suggestions:

- ✓ Raise the bed.
- ✓ Change doorknobs and hardware on bedroom furnishings.
- ✓ Install grab bars near the bed and at areas where dressing occurs.
- ✓ Remove or add furniture. Consider adding a chair for dressing. Bedrooms can be areas of congestion where tripping hazards are an ongoing issue. If this is the case for you, it's very wise to make more room for your preferred travel routes around your bedroom.
- ✓ Ensure there's an easy location for placing soiled or dirty clothes. Soiled or dirty clothes are a common source of clutter on the backs of chairs or tripping hazards on the floor. If you don't already have a routine to deal with this problem, adapt your bedroom to keep it uncluttered and free from tripping hazards.
- ✓ Ensure sufficient lights are in convenient locations for reading, washroom visits, and winding down before going to sleep.

9. Bathroom

Bathrooms can be hazardous and difficult zones as we age. Maintaining balance as we close our eyes to wash our hair, getting off a toilet seat, and standing up from a sitting position in a bathtub are a few of the tasks that require a measure of physical fitness to do safely and securely. Adaptive changes to your bathroom can help you with these and many other things in your bathroom. The following are some suggestions for adapting your bathroom:

- ✓ Add grab bars around the tub, shower, and toilet. Grab bars help with balance while washing your hair, and soaping and rinsing. They definitely help you to stand up from a sitting position on a toilet or in a bathtub. In some cases, you need a grab bar for a sitting position and one installed higher for a standing position. It's important to position them at the right height for how they will be used and it's also important that they're fastened securely into structural and stable elements of the surrounding building materials. If you're unsure what's stable and structural, consult a professional. You also need to be sure to maintain the integrity of the surrounding building materials by not penetrating moisture/water barriers without taking the proper corrective or restoration measures.
- ✓ Use a nonslip mat in your shower and/or bathtub.

✓ Ensure you use a bath mat with rubber backing. Don't use towels placed on the floor because they can slide causing a fall.

✓ Replace fixtures if the style of fixture is difficult to use. A single-lever faucet with the hot-cold controlled by one push or pull of the lever is easiest to use for arthritic hands and fingers.

✓ Replace cabinet hardware and doorknobs with easy-to-use styles.

✓ Replace or remove mechanical or magnetic cabinet clasps if they are troublesome.

✓ Turn down the hot water heater to a safe level (about 120 degrees Fahrenheit or 49 degrees Celsius). It is safer to risk running out of hot water than to risk burning or scalding because a temperature setting is too high.

✓ Add a seat to the shower. This usually requires that you also replace the shower faucet with a handheld type. It's important to get a safe seat or stool that is stable and easy to use. There are both fold-up seats that can be fastened onto the surrounding structure and portable stools that sit on the tub or shower enclosure floor.

✓ Replace showerhead with a handheld/mountable type. Handheld showerheads go hand in hand with shower stools or seats. The stream of water can be directed where it's needed and in any direction. Handheld showerheads are also very useful when mobility, flexibility, and balance become an issue. Being able to sit or stand while directing the flow of water greatly reduces the need for shower gymnastics while trying to get at those hard to reach areas!

✓ Raise the toilet or replace your toilet seat with a raised seat. This can greatly help the process of standing up or sitting down on a toilet. It's especially helpful for those individuals who are beginning to lose leg strength. You can purchase a heightened seat or renovate the toilet structure to create a heightened toilet.

10. Stairs

Stairs can become very hazardous as we age due the increased potential for falls as our balance, strength, dexterity, and vision declines. Although we need to be more careful around stairs as we age, there are adaptations that can be done to help us navigate stairways in our home. The following suggestions can help make your stairways safer:

- ✓ Remove carpeting or secure loose carpeting. Anything that changes the consistency of risers or creates instability underfoot needs to be repaired or secured as quickly as possible.

- ✓ Add extra handrails. When it comes to stairs, more handholds will make stairs easier and safer to navigate. Sometimes the handrail is only on one side of the staircase if it's against a wall. It is advisable to have handrails on both sides of a staircase.

- ✓ Repair broken or insecure steps, handrails, and handrail-support structures. Anything that wobbles or is insecure underfoot can throw you off balance. This is very hazardous when it occurs on a stairway. Make sure broken or insecure steps or handrails are fixed or replaced immediately on discovering the problem.

- ✓ Add reflective strips or high contrast strips to aid vision and depth perception.

- ✓ Increase or add lighting.

- ✓ Place a "stop" sign at the top of stairways to remind you to stop, focus, go slowly, and be careful. Although a stop sign at the top of a stairway might seem a bit drastic, it's an important reminder that danger lies ahead. It brings one to a place of stopping and then proceeding with caution, having recognized the danger ahead. I see many signs on the ski hill "Danger — Cliff" or "Danger — Steep Terrain"; trust me, many of those signs have saved my bacon!

11. Furnishings

Furnishings can be adapted in many ways to increase safety and comfort as we age. Low seating is fine for sitting down because gravity is working with you when you sit but it can be very difficult for standing up because gravity is working against you. By simply opting for higher seating, your furnishings can become much more user friendly. There are other adaptations that can be made to your furnishings as you age which can help you age more safely in your home:

- ✓ Raise seats, chairs, and couches. As previously mentioned, creating a raised base, building or buying raised castors or floor protectors, or even changing short legs to tall legs are adaptations that making getting up from sitting easier.

- ✓ Replace furnishings with sharp corners or at least cover the corners with padding or bumpers. Some furniture really hurts when you bump into it. If you have sharp corners that are a nuisance, now is the time to make the simple adaptation by getting some padding or rubber bumpers in place.

12. Garages

Garages have many different uses. They can be workshops or set up to pursue hobbies such as building models, woodworking, or painting. They can be excellent storage areas and often double as garden sheds. Whatever you use your garage for there are countless adaptations that can make your garage safer and easier to use. Here are a few suggestions:

- ✓ Use some visual/physical aids to help you park your car in the best place every time. Use reflective tape on the edges of the garage door openings to help you better gauge your position and help with depth perception. Position a piece of wood (two by four or two by six) where you want your front wheels to be. Hang a tennis ball to gauge the stopping spot when you park. When the ball touches your windshield right in front of your face, you're parked correctly.

- ✓ Install or buy shelving to help organize your garage.

- ✓ Install ready-made workbenches or cupboards.

- ✓ Install hooks and create areas to hang items.

- ✓ Add lighting or provide a hook for mobile lighting.

13. Additional Changes

There's an increasingly wide array of products and adaptive resources designed to make our lives simpler, safer, and more comfortable as we age. If you want to age well and safely in your home, spend some time educating yourself about the wide variety of things available to you. This book has only touched on some of the many useful items and resources that could make aging safely in your home much more pleasant. A few other suggestions, not previously mentioned are as follows:

- ✓ Phone with features such as large numbers, volume control, and caller identification.

- ✓ Message or memory boards. A message or memory board allows you to write things down such as groceries that are needed, minor repairs that need to be done, or appointments.

- ✓ Porta-potties and bedpans.

14. Top Ten Adaptations

There is such an enormous volume of adaptations for the home owner who wants to remain in place as long as possible that we felt a Top 10 Checklist would be useful to focus on some of the more important items. Although this list is open to interpretation, we feel the following items in Checklist 7 are among the most important adaptations for aging safely in your home.

Rethink functionality of your home. The way it is now is not necessarily the way it should be if you want to age safely in your home.

Checklist 7
TOP TEN HOME ADAPTATIONS

	Task	Completed
1.	Get rid of throw rugs.	
2.	Add more lighting including installing motion lights.	
3.	Install indoor and outdoor handrails	
4.	Install grab bars in the bathroom.	
5.	Frequently review your bathroom functionality and make the necessary adaptations as the need arises.	
6.	Frequently review your kitchen functionality and make the necessary adaptations as the need arises.	
7.	Find or create more storage space.	
8.	De-clutter to get rid of things you no longer use. This also creates wider, safer travel routes in your home.	
9.	Install smoke and carbon monoxide detectors. Remember to check the batteries at least once a year.	
10.	Frequently review Checklist 6: Rate Your Home in Chapter 5 and make the appropriate changes when issues are noted.	

chapter 8

Renovate Your Home

Do you want to renovate your home to help you remain living there? Do you worry about the time, cost, and effort required to complete a renovation? Do you wonder what sorts of things will be helpful to age safely in your home? Do you need a bit of guidance to help you get started with a renovation project?

Renovating a home is a big job that often requires professional help. Getting the right professionals for the job is something that requires preparation, gathering, and organizing of information and due diligence. You, the home owner, are responsible for getting the right team in place to make your renovation run smoothly. This can seem a daunting task if you're unfamiliar with the construction industry. Luckily, we're in the information age and much of the information you require is readily at your fingertips. Despite the fact renovating your home for aging safely can be a substantial undertaking, it doesn't need to be an aggravating experience. You just need to take the right steps to get a good professional renovator working for you with a fair contract that will protect you.

1. Renovation Costs and Timelines

Whenever someone is considering a renovation, one of the first questions is: How much will it cost? This is certainly an important question but without a very specific plan in place, "how much" is very difficult to determine. It's often better to work backwards, starting with your budget. Renovations are expensive. How much you have to spend determines how much can be done which ultimately can answer the question of whether it's wise to begin your renovation.

Generally speaking, renovations are more expensive than you thought they were going to be. Just ask anyone who's ever done a renovation. It's important to feel financially comfortable with your commitment on costs.

The same can be said of timelines. Generally speaking, renovations almost always take longer than you think they will take. Most contractors will give you a best case scenario estimate on timeline. Inevitably, orders, materials, and/or labor will have delays or problems, so your timeline gets increased. It's wise to allow for more time than estimated to complete the job.

The bottom line regarding costs and timelines is that they need to be established using accurate and specific information. When costs and timelines are established, they need to be controlled properly through skilled communication and competent project management.

Before getting started with any renovation project, you need a clear and specific idea of what needs to be done and you need a budget. This is the starting point for any renovation project. It's advisable to get professionals involved right away to help you sort the possibilities for your budget and design ideas. It's important to have both realistic ideas and expectations regarding costs. When it comes to renovations, the sky is the limit on both what can be done and what it may cost.

When the preliminary ideas and budgets have been deemed workable and realistic, it's time to get a good designer and a good contractor working for you. The process for choosing these professionals should be organized, well-documented, and well-researched. This important early phase of your renovation will take work, effort, and possibly some money but getting the right people working for you from the beginning is essential.

2. Choosing a Designer

A good designer will help you clarify and document your vision and ideas for your renovation. The designer can help you achieve a project that is cost effective in making a home more functional, comfortable, and safe. When considering renovations, some people are very clear about what they need and want, while others only have a general idea. Designers create documents that clarify all aspects of a renovation project. This, in turn, will enable contractors to accurately prepare cost estimates and ultimately complete the renovation according to the client's wishes. A successful renovation starts with a clear, well-documented set of plans and specifications, which is why a good designer is a great place to begin any renovation project.

When a renovation involves aging safely in your home, a good designer can incorporate the best practices of universal design, which means designing products and physical spaces that consider the needs of persons of all ages and abilities or disabilities. Universal design includes best practices for designing for functionality, comfort, and safety for persons of any age or physical capability. If you want to age safely in your home, a designer who understands universal design is your best resource.

2.1 Tips for finding a good designer

The following tips can help you get a good designer working for you:

- ✓ Ask for referrals from family, friends, and neighbors. Word-of-mouth advertising is almost always the best way to find a good designer.

- ✓ Try to be fair and balanced when interviewing designers by giving them exactly the same questions and information. Write down your questions prior to contacting them. Give all your candidates a similar opportunity to sell themselves or convince you that they're the right designer for you.

- ✓ Ask whether they have experience with universal design.

- ✓ If you're not sure what you need or want, good designers should make you feel like they'll be able to help you sort that out on your initial "free" consultation.

- ✓ Have a discussion with a minimum of three designers before choosing the one you want.

- ✓ Ask for credentials.

- ✓ Check references.
- ✓ Some designers will also monitor construction or act as a project manager or coordinator (for a fee). If this is something you want, ask them if that's a service they provide, and make sure you understand the costs for those services.
- ✓ Be clear about the drawing, specification, and permits package. You will need a complete set of working drawings for construction. Specifications will vary depending on the size and scope of the project. Specifications about products, makes, and models will enable more accurate cost estimates from your contractors at the bidding stage. You must also sort out who will secure the permit, if a building permit is required.
- ✓ Check the Better Business Bureau for information and ratings about the designers under consideration.

You'll need to sit down with your designer to discuss the following issues:

- ✓ Budget.
- ✓ "Wants" for your new renovation.
- ✓ "Needs" for your new renovation.
- ✓ Physical disabilities.
- ✓ Aesthetic/appearance concerns.
- ✓ Resale concerns.
- ✓ Involvement level. This means your intentions for choosing tiles, fixtures, colors, and whatever else needs to be decided on for the renovation. Some clients will trust their designer to sort out these issues and others will prefer to choose everything themselves.
- ✓ Communication procedures and expectations. Communication is crucial on a renovation project. It is useful to have an agreed on method and time frame for how you'll communicate and when.
- ✓ Design package and cost.
- ✓ You need to have an agreement, in writing, regarding the exact inclusions and exclusions of the design package. In other words, you need to know what you're getting from the designer and how much it will cost. It's a separate contract from the one for the builder or renovator. Make sure you read the contract,

and if you are having trouble understanding anything in it, ask someone you trust for help.

3. Choosing a Contractor

Choosing a contractor is a very important task when considering major renovations. There has been a great deal of negative publicity in recent years about the motives and workmanship of many contractors. It's true, there are some bad contractors, but it's more accurate to acknowledge most are good and well intentioned. The important issue is: how do you hire one of the really good contractors?

Getting one of the good contractors is often a result of being a smart customer. When hiring a contractor, *you* are in control of who gets hired. Do your homework. That's the best way to get a good contractor and a well-written contract that protects you. Hiring a good contractor is really not that difficult. Problems arise when customers take shortcuts on the selection process and the process of getting a fair and balanced contract in place and signed. It's very important that you read the contract, and if you are having trouble understanding anything in it, ask someone you trust for help.

3.1 Tips for finding a good contractor

Here's a checklist for selecting a contractor:

- ✓ Thinking "cheap" and "fast" doesn't mean you will get "good" work.
- ✓ Ask for referrals from family, friends, or neighbors.
- ✓ Give exactly the same set of drawings, instructions, and specifications to each contractor who is being considered to do the work. Be as specific as possible.
- ✓ Sort out what you need done before hiring a contractor. Hiring a designer is money well spent if you're not sure. Some contractors are design/build contractors but beware that there might be some bias on materials and design if you hire someone who does both design and construction. It's not necessarily a bad thing, but it's something to remember, especially if they're pushing for a certain type of tile or flooring which might be left over from a previous job.
- ✓ Get at least three quotes.
- ✓ Ask for credentials.

- ✓ Check references.
- ✓ Speak to the contractors and get a feel for who they are and what they're all about. Don't be offended if prospective contractors are asking lots of questions. Good contractors should have questions to help them quote your job accurately.
- ✓ Check the Better Business Bureau for information and ratings about the contractors under consideration.

If you don't feel comfortable organizing your own renovation, work through an owner's representative who can be a son, daughter, trusted friend, or even someone you hire for that purpose.

Most contractors have become very good negotiators due to the nature of their business. Everything in a contract is negotiable so if you're uncomfortable with the process of negotiation, you'd be well advised to get help with this part of your renovation project.

4. Contracts

When you've worked through a well-organized process to find the right designer followed by a similar process to find the right contractor, you'll need to get a well-written contract in place. Don't sign anything until you're confident that it's a good contract for you. Most contractors will have a standard contractual document that they use for all their jobs. Don't hesitate to consult a lawyer at this stage to ensure you get a contract that will protect you.

Remember, a standard contract from a contractor is usually written to protect the contractor. There will usually be some changes required to help make the contract fair for both parties. Important parts of the contract that need documentation and examination are as follows:

- ✓ Name of the contract, for example, Bathroom Renovation for Ray's Home.
- ✓ Names of the contractor and client.
- ✓ Address of where the work will be done.
- ✓ Description of the work to be done. This part of the contract needs to be very specific. There should be specific references to design documents, materials, makes and models, and workmanship. This section needs to thoroughly and completely describe what needs to be done. Depending on the size of the renovation, it can be an extensive and lengthy portion of the contract.

- ✓ Time frame for work completion.

- ✓ Payment details such as amounts to be paid and dates they should be paid.

- ✓ There needs to be a procedure in place for making changes to the agreed on contract.

- ✓ Specific inclusions and standard clauses you may need or may be required by state, provincial, or territorial law. This is where contracts can get messy. Different areas require specific inclusions. Some examples of these items are warranties, conflict-resolution clauses, and cancellation rights. If you're unfamiliar with construction contracts, consulting a lawyer is advisable.

- ✓ Signatures of the contractor, client, and witnesses.

Do your due diligence at the contract stage, before you sign.

5. Renovation Ideas

When considering a renovation, it's important to understand the process. You can't jump to a pleasant vision of your renovated home and all the comfort and functionality of your vision without acknowledging and accepting the reality of embarking on a renovation. There will be disruption, costs, and the possibility of unforeseen problems. Think in terms of investing lots of energy and resources in exchange for grand rewards. That will place you in the right frame of mind.

There are many possibilities for renovating your home to help you age safely. The following suggestions are intended to get you thinking about the possibilities. Although the possibilities are endless, renovating certain areas of your home can be especially helpful in your senior years. The following suggestions are areas and ideas that have proven very helpful to others who needed to make changes in order to age safely in their homes.

5.1 Travel routes and flooring

Preventing falls is a good place to begin when considering a renovation. As we age, we become more prone to balance, strength, and co-ordination problems. Here are some suggestions:

- ✓ To help navigate travel routes, renovate to include more handrails or grab bars.

- ✓ Eliminate door thresholds or at the very least paint or stain thresholds a contrasting color.

- ✓ Widening doors and travel routes may be necessary if the home owner is using a wheelchair or anticipating the use of a wheelchair.

- ✓ Outdoors, ramps can be built as an alternate to stairways.

- ✓ Depending on the terrain outside your home, you may want to recontour your yard to eliminate steep areas or stairways that are difficult to navigate. Uneven concrete can be leveled or broken and re-poured.

- ✓ Areas where you might slide or where you might catch your foot and stumble are good places to think about renovating. Flooring can be replaced especially if there are slippery areas in your home that are not stable and secure underfoot. Flooring wholesalers and retailers can determine which flooring types are best to reduce or eliminate slippery floors.

- ✓ Travel routes can be improved by having more or better lighting. Motion lights are often used outdoors but they can also be helpful around your indoor travel routes.

5.2 Kitchens

Kitchens are typically heavily used areas in a home. When you factor in prep time and eating time, it's worthwhile considering a kitchen renovation. As we age, the way we use our kitchen changes. Years of using our kitchen has taught us what works and what doesn't work. A kitchen renovation has so many possibilities:

- ✓ Chopping vegetables while sitting down.

- ✓ Turning on your faucet simply by touching it!

- ✓ Preparing most of your meals in a microwave or toaster oven.

- ✓ Reworking how garbage is handled in your kitchen for recycling and composting.

- ✓ Downsizing your kitchen so that using it requires less movement.

- ✓ Adding a large freezer so you make fewer visits to the supermarket for food.

- ✓ Making the kitchen wheelchair useable and ergonomically versatile.

5.3 Bathrooms

The bathroom should be a primary area of focus for renovating to help you age safely in your home. Many falls occur in the bathroom for various reasons. Issues that contribute to falling in bathrooms include:

- ✓ Water on floor. Renovating to minimize water pooling on floor.

- ✓ Strength and balance when sitting or standing in the shower and/or bath tub. Renovating bathrooms to include adequate grab bars for different positions in a bathtub, shower, toilet, dressing, or grooming area is very worthwhile.

- ✓ Strength and balance when using the toilets. There are some very sophisticated toilet and bidet units that are both comfortable and hygienic. Redesigning a bathroom to allow for more physiological advantage regarding strength issues can be very helpful.

- ✓ Fatigue due to the time of day these areas are most frequently used. Getting bright lighting will help to keep seniors alert during the times of day when fatigue can cause problems.

- ✓ Complications due to illness or administering medicine.

It's often advisable to relocate bathrooms to more convenient areas of your home. There are solutions to most problems and a good bathroom designer can help make your life easier.

5.4 One-level living space

If you want to age safely in a home that has more than one level, you should really consider renovating for one-level living. Moving back and forth through multiple levels of a home greatly increases your risk for falls, not to mention the energy drain if navigating stairs has become difficult. Although getting your cooking, bathing, sleeping, and living spaces on one level might be costly, the payoff in the long run might be worth it. As you age, having to navigate through only one level of your home makes so much sense. The other levels can always be there for kids, grandkids, friends, and other visitors.

5.5 Bedroom with en suite

Not all homes have bedrooms with en suites. It is convenient to have a bathroom attached to your bedroom. Those middle-of-the-night bathroom breaks become safer and more convenient, plus there's an enhanced feeling of safety at times of illness knowing your bathroom is just steps away. It doesn't need to be a large bathroom to provide safety and convenience. A small space for a vanity and toilet is all that's required.

5.6 Heating and cooling systems

As we age, we become more sensitive to temperature issues. One of the simplest renovations for keeping more heat in your home is to add insulation in your ceiling/attic space. Upgrading heating and cooling systems can make a big difference, especially for older homes. Technology has made these sorts of mechanical systems more efficient. The way air moves throughout your home can be a difficult thing to figure out so consulting a heating and cooling specialist is advisable. These are some common problems to consider fixing:

- ✓ Inadequate insulation.
- ✓ Air escaping through older windows and doors that have damaged seals.
- ✓ Chimneys letting warm air escape the home.
- ✓ Vermin that have damaged ductwork in the heating and cooling systems.

Whatever the case, renovating to accommodate a more temperate environment can be comforting and save you money in the long run.

5.7 Window and door replacements

There are many different reasons to renovate doors and windows. Window and door replacements sometimes go hand in hand with trying to get heating and cooling issues under control. Windows and doors can also have a significant impact on noise issues by replacing or upgrading them. It's also possible to change the styles of doors and windows to make them easier to use or to provide a heightened level of home security.

Depending on the condition of your doors and windows, refurbishing whatever you currently have in place can be very helpful. Re-caulking, lubricating hinges, fixing cranks and levers, changing weather stripping, and upgrading door locks and handles can make a significant difference. It might be expensive to focus on windows and doors but it can certainly enhance your comfort level.

5.8 Stair climbers, escalators, and elevators

Sometimes we just love our homes so much, we want to stay despite the barrier that stairs can create. In these situations, a renovation to find an alternate means of traveling from floor to floor is a possibility. This type of renovation is for the financially secure because it can be expensive and doesn't always increase resale value. There are a number of options for elevators, stair climbers, and escalators. These types of renovations can accommodate able-bodied seniors or wheelchair-bound seniors.

5.9 Suite conversions

Living in a large home that has enough room for multiple tenants creates opportunities to enhance your income, increase your circle of friends, and the ability to give back to your community. Converting part of your home to suites for tenants or even creating something more suitable for yourself while renting out another portion of your home can have many benefits.

Many years ago, I rented a room from a retired woman and I still feel indebted to her because I was a struggling student at the time. She helped me with her gift of giving back to her community.

5.10 Garages

Garages can be a great space to pursue hobbies such as auto repair and maintenance, model building, or other hobbies. I knew a retired gentleman in Ontario who turned his garage into a hockey museum and skate-sharpening center. He took donations for community causes in exchange for sharpening skates. The place was always busy with its wood-burning fireplace and free coffee. People would stop by for 20 minutes, have a coffee, and get their skates sharpened while swapping hockey stories. This man built a social network, gave back to his community, and kept active both mentally and physically. It was uniquely fantastic!

Evidently, garages can be a great place to help you age actively and safely. Adding insulation and heating or reconfiguring the garage to accommodate a favorite activity or hobby are great options.

Sometimes, an automobile is no longer needed, at which time the garage can be renovated for extra living space or even as an income-generating space, such as a laneway house. Laneway houses are an interesting new development in urban living. They are separate buildings on properties zoned as single-family residences that provide owners an opportunity for income-generating rental suites. Garages are either converted or torn down and rebuilt into a laneway house. By wisely choosing the right tenant, a home owner can create not only a source of income but also a source of help for yard work or minor repairs and maintenance.

6. Top Five Renovations

Worksheet 3 will help you analyze and prioritize the renovations you need to comfortably and safely age in your home.

Worksheet 3
TOP FIVE RENOVATIONS

Location	Notes on What Needs to be Done
Bathroom: We tend to use a bathroom more frequently as we age and it's an area of the home that becomes more difficult to use as time goes on. Consider renovating the bathroom first to ensure falling hazards are minimized.	
One-level living: Eliminate stairs and elevation changes to prevent falls.	
Flooring: Eliminate uneven sections of your travel routes to help prevent trips, slips, and falls.	
Kitchen: Make it a more efficient space for preparing meals and other activities you enjoy doing in that area of your home.	
Mobility upgrades: Allow for wheelchair accessibility or install mechanical devices to assist you in climbing stairs or for traveling from floor to floor.	

chapter 9

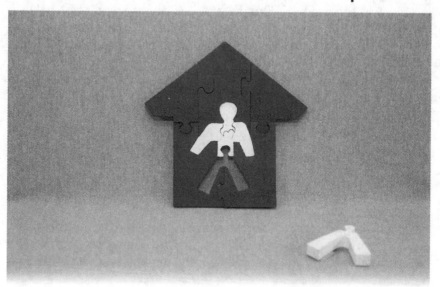

Prevent Falls

Do you know seniors who have fallen in their home? Are you worried about falling in your home? Do you know that most falls are preventable? Would you like to know how to prevent falling in your home?

An 80-something-year-old neighbor recently complained about the fact that she always seems to land on her face whenever she falls. She seemed resigned to the fact she might fall but annoyed by the fact she always seemed to end up on her face. I know of two falls she had recently, one of which resulted in a couple of black eyes. Her husband, who's probably 90, had a bad fall while putting up Christmas lights a few years ago. I feel so bad for these kindly neighbors. They're just trying to maintain their independence but these types of falls accelerate the aging process making aging in place more difficult. I have witnessed a remarkable deterioration of independent living capacity from these neighbors after their falls. I cringe every time I hear about elders falling because falls are both mentally and physically bruising. It can be very difficult to recover after a fall. Prevention is clearly the key.

My two neighbors could have prevented their falls by recognizing and taking the necessary precautions to avoid the falls that occurred. One fall was the result of climbing a ladder. Unfortunately, age, balance issues, and the inherent dangers of ladders should have prevented my 90-year-old neighbor from attempting to install his Christmas lights. His wife was tripped up by a throw rug which probably should have been eliminated from the home decor because throw rugs can be dangerous tripping hazards as our balance and foot dexterity decreases with age. It's easy to say in retrospect, but there's a valuable lesson to be learned. We all need to be prevention-oriented as we age to avoid the debilitating effects of falls and the complications such falls bring into our lives.

Preventing falls is a combination of physical capability and keeping your living space free from hazards. You need to be at your physical best to be alert, balanced, and strong. You also need to be constantly on the lookout for tripping or slipping hazards; however, spotting the hazard isn't enough. You need to fix it by eliminating or at least minimizing it.

Falls by seniors are a very big issue in North America. The statistics for falling among senior citizens are staggering. According to Health Canada, "Every year, one in three Canadian seniors will fall at least once. Hip fractures are the most common type of fall injury among seniors, and about 20 percent of injury-related deaths among seniors can be traced back to a fall."[1]

According to the Centers for Disease Control and Prevention, "in 2002, more than 12,800 people over age 65 died and 1.6 million were treated in emergency departments because of falls."[2]

1. Problems and Solutions

The good news is there are preventive measures that can and should be taken to ensure you're not a part of the alarming statistics regarding seniors and the devastating results of falling. Worksheet 4 will help you to look for common falling and slipping hazards and how to do some quick fixes.

---

1 "Seniors and Aging — Preventing Falls in and around Your Home," Health Canada, accessed February 2015. http://www.hc-sc.gc.ca/hl-vs/iyh-vsv/life-vie/fp-pc-eng.php
2 "Check for Safety: A Home Fall Prevention Checklist for Older Adults," National Center for Injury Prevention and Control, Centers for Disease Control and Prevention, accessed February 2015. http://www.cdc.gov/ncipc/pub-res/toolkit/checklistforsafety.htm

Worksheet 4
PREVENT FALLS AND SLIPS

Problem	Solution	Notes
Outside the Home		
Poor visibility at night.	Ensure there are adequate lights or install motion lights.	
Tripping hazards caused by yard clutter, garden tools, or other outdoor equipment or recreation items.	Take the good housekeeping vigilance outside. Put away all items when not using them.	
Uneven ground, paving, or transition zones.	Level ground, repave, or install handrails. You can also bring attention to these areas by using bright paint or contrasting colors.	
Slippery conditions due to snow, ice, or leaves.	Ensure stairs and walkways are kept clear of hazardous conditions and install handrails.	
Floors, Stairs, and Travel Routes		
Home furnishings and decor creates traffic-flow problems and tripping or loss of balance issues.	Rearrange furniture and home decor to create easily accessible traffic routes that ensure ease of travel and maintenance of balance.	
Area or throw rugs create a slipping or tripping hazard.	Eliminate throw rugs. If your sense of style refuses to eliminate the rugs, use double-sided tape or nonskid backing to stabilize area or throw rugs. Eliminate rugs with tassels or fringe. Ensure corners of the rugs aren't riding up.	
Wires and cords create tripping hazard.	Move all wires and cords against the walls. Use extension cords to place them against walls or rearrange furnishings and appliances to better locations for outlet use or rewire outlets.	
Tripping and slipping hazards are left on floors and travel routes.	Always put things away, paying particular attention to keeping floors and travel routes clear.	
Lighting or shadowing makes visibility and depth perception a problem.	Ensure travel routes and stairs are adequately lit to maximize vision. Install night-lights in any areas traveled at night.	
Difficult travel areas create balance hazards.	Ensure stairs, uneven outdoor areas, and slippery zones have adequate and secure handrails and grab bars.	

Living Areas		
Transition areas between rooms and through doorways are not clearly defined.	Ensure transitions are clearly marked, defined, and visible. Install grab bars (if necessary) to provide stability support where walking surfaces have irregularities or transitions.	
Cluttered living space creates tripping hazard.	De-clutter and habitually return items to storage places.	
Kitchen		
Pots, pans, and utensils are difficult to reach.	Store frequently used items in easy to reach locations. Reconfigure cabinet space and storage areas to make accessibility easier.	
Floors become slippery when wet due to water or spills.	Always wipe up spills immediately; have a mop or towel easily accessible for this purpose.	
High cabinet areas are difficult to reach.	Store infrequently used (light) items in high cabinets. Use a stable step stool with a safety rail to reach high places.	
Heavy items are difficult to move.	Store heavy items in lower cupboards or on convenient counter space.	
Bedrooms		
Cluttered or poorly lit travel route to bathroom.	De-clutter travel route to bathroom and install a night-light.	
Difficulty with balance when dressing.	Provide chair and/or install grab bars to provide seating or assist with balance during dressing.	
Bathrooms		
Slippery conditions caused by water on the floor.	Wipe up water on floors right away. Have an old towel specifically for that purpose in a convenient, easy-to-access location.	
Slippery conditions in tub and shower areas.	Install grip tape, grip decals, and/or rubber nonskid bathmat in tub/shower. Install grab bars to assist with balance and for sitting and standing.	
Balance problems in the shower.	Install grab bars to assist with balance and/or get a shower stool and change shower nozzle to a handheld type.	

Balance and strength issues when using the toilet.	Install a raised toilet, raised seat, and/or grab bars at toilet areas.	
Difficulty getting in and out of the bathtub and/or shower.	Install grab bars or install a different type of bathing unit such as a walk-in tub or handicap shower.	
Personal Considerations		
Unprepared to move around safely in your home.	Remove reading glasses; ensure you're feeling balanced and ready to move before beginning; don't rush when moving around your home.	
Feeling dizzy or unsteady when getting out of a bed or chair.	Get up slowly or in stages when getting out of bed. Install grab bars where getting up occurs. Begin moving your legs before getting up from a chair.	
Stationary or wall mounted phones create a tripping hazard when rushing to answer them.	Use a wireless or mobile device and always have it near you or inform people that you will return calls at your convenience.	
Seasonal issues such as snow removal or holiday decorating difficulties.	Ask for help for any difficult tasks.	

2. Ladder Safety

Recently, a friend of mine, who doesn't like heights or ladders, asked me to have a look at a broken eaves trough and downspout at his house. The broken piece was at a corner of the upper roof on a two-story house. As a renovator, I've been on ladders countless times but not recently. In fact, I haven't been on a ladder for the past five years. I want to tell you something important: Age and the passing of time really does change things. While having a look at the gutter problem, I discovered I wasn't nearly as stable or comfortable at the top of an extension ladder as I had been in the past. I realized that the things I used to do on ladders will be more challenging as I age. In the case of my friend's broken gutter, I had to make the difficult admission that I wasn't able to fix his problem because I was no longer comfortable working at the top of a ladder. That was a difficult admission but it was the right thing to do.

Ladders can be a very hazardous tool as we age. It's very important to feel safe, stable, and comfortable when using a ladder. Although I don't feel as good on a ladder as I once did, over the years I have certainly learned a thing or two about using them. Think carefully about your suitability to work on ladders before attempting to use this potentially hazardous tool.

2.1 Tips for using a ladder safely

Ladders are safer when used with another person to help stabilize. The other person can also be on the lookout for possible loss of balance or other safety hazards. Although ladders can be a very useful tool, as we age they become a tool that can contribute to an increased potential for falls. Make sure you're a fit senior with good balance before attempting to use a ladder.

If you must use a ladder, and you are definitely capable, including feeling safe, stable, and comfortable, here are a few tips about ladder use:

- ✓ Use the three-point rule: Two feet and one hand or two hands and one foot should *always* be in contact with the ladder.
- ✓ *Always* face the ladder holding onto the rungs, and not the sides.
- ✓ Use ladders during the daylight hours in calm, dry weather conditions.
- ✓ *Always* place the ladder on a firm, solid, and level surface, making sure that the contact points of the base of the ladder aren't able to slide or skid.
- ✓ As a general rule of thumb, an extension ladder should be placed one foot away from the surface it rests against for every four feet of height.
- ✓ *Always* take one step at a time whether going up or coming down a ladder.
- ✓ Use a tool belt or waist pouch when carrying or using tools while on a ladder.
- ✓ Keep your body between the rails (sides) of a ladder.
- ✓ *Never* lean or overreach; instead, reposition the ladder.

3. Final Thoughts on Preventing Falls

Nobody wants to fall so when it happens, it usually takes us by surprise. To avoid and prevent the surprising and unfortunate occurrence of a fall, you need to keep a few things in mind:

- ✓ Keep physically fit; this is the best thing a person can do to prevent falls.

- ✓ Use common sense. A few examples include staying off slippery surfaces; wearing stable, nonslippery, supportive shoes; and never standing on anything with wheels.

- ✓ Be mindful about medications, especially those that might have the side effects of making you sleepy or drowsy.

- ✓ Get regular checkups from your health practitioners. Good vision and adequate foot and leg mobility are just two of the important issues to be monitored by your family doctor.

- ✓ Slow down and take it easy. Whether getting up from sleep, getting up from a chair, or moving from room to room, take your time.

- ✓ Be aware of the common locations for falling which include cluttered and/or crowded areas, uneven surfaces, stairs, doorways, areas prone to wetness or spills, unguarded heightened areas, and ladders.

- ✓ Use safety aids (if required) such as glasses, hearing aids, canes, and walkers.

- ✓ Wear a security alarm bracelet for an added measure of protection if you are prone to falls or worried about falling. Emergency help will be just a touch away.

Conclusion

Our book's last chapter is about preventing falls. There's irony in the fact that many seniors' final chapter in their home starts with a fall. Physical complications resulting from falls can force a senior to relocate even when he or she is not ready or willing to do so. But we believe most falls can be prevented by taking the holistic approach to personal and home adaptations that we have recommended in this book.

We want to highlight several key points about how to age safely in your home:

1. It requires an ongoing cycle of evaluating, monitoring, and adapting.

2. You need both the energy and the willingness to make the required adaptations.

3. It can be more manageable if you make it a team effort.

4. You need to monitor and take care of yourself physically, emotionally, socially, mentally, and spiritually.

5. You need to monitor and take care of your home through assessing, creating comfort, adapting, renovating, and protecting against falls.

This book is essentially about evaluating and expanding your capacity to age safely in your home. We truly believe that if you can make the adaptations we've recommended you *will* be able to age safely in your home. We hope this book creates a framework for discussion and action because we want you to live your life safely in your own home, on your own terms, and by intention.

appendix

Signs That It's Time to Move

This information is for a senior's family or innermost circle of friends who are concerned about their loved one's ability to age safely in his or her home. Use this book as a guideline to evaluate the current status of the person's health and wellness as described in each chapter.

If the Rate Yourself evaluations in this book reveal a majority of negative responses, see what you can do to encourage and inspire your loved one to make the personal and/or home adaptations needed to keep him or her healthy, well, and safe in his or her home. If your loved one is incapable of making the suggested adaptations, unwilling to accept help, or not able to afford the required professional assistance needed to age safely in his or her home, then it is time for the person to relocate. Use Checklist 8 to help you assess your loved one's situation.

Crisis signals must not be ignored. Contact your local health authority as soon as you notice any of the following situations:

- Frequent emergency room visits.
- Reports from police, medical teams, and/or neighbors about the senior.
- Depression or suicidal tendencies.

Signs of deteriorating conditions indicate a change is needed. Because each senior's situation is unique, this change can mean obtaining adequate informal care, hiring professional assistance, and/or relocating to a more suitable housing location. Be aware of the following signs of deteriorating conditions:

- The senior cannot safely be left alone.
- A single senior is becoming socially isolated from family, friends, and/or community.
- Family or other close members are experiencing caregiver burnout.
- The senior begins to experience delusions or a distorted sense of reality.
- The senior or the family are dissatisfied with the quality of caregiver services.

Checklist 8
ASSESS YOUR LOVED ONE'S SITUATION

Question	Never	Occasionally	Frequently
How often has the senior fallen in the last six months?			
How often has the senior been to the emergency room in the last six months?			
Has the senior experienced the loss of a loved one in the last year?			
How often in the last six months has the senior shown signs of depression?			
Does the senior need assistance in bathing or dressing?			
Does the senior need assistance with meal preparation?			
How often does the senior miss taking prescribed medication?			
Will the senior accept "outside help" for personal and home care?			
Does the senior need assistance paying his or her monthly bills?			
How often is the senior missing social events?			
How often do situations arise where a family member or close friend is unable to assist the senior?			
How often has a family member lost time from work in the past six months to deal with the senior's crisis?			
How much free family time is used to take care of the senior's needs?			

Source: Checklist 8 is used with permission from the Canadian Initiative for Elder Planning Studies. Please note minor changes have been made to it and approved by the Canadian Initiative for Elder Planning Studies.

Resources

1. Websites

Canada Mortgage and Housing Corporation

Provides information on accessible and adaptable housing and financial assistance programs.

www.cmhc-schl.gc.ca

Eldercare Locator

Connects seniors to community services.

www.eldercare.gov

Government of Canada: Seniors

Provides information to help seniors age in place.

www.seniors.gc.ca

Health Canada

Offers practical tips for healthy eating, injury prevention, oral health, physical activity, and smoking cessation for seniors.

www.hc-sc.gc.ca

Help Guide

A nonprofit organization that provides a guide to better emotional and mental health for seniors.

www.helpguide.org

National Aging in Place Council

Provides information to help you age in place.

www.ageinplace.org

National Association of Home Builders

Provides information for aging in place remodeling.

www.nahb.org

National Institute on Aging Senior Health

Offers easy to read alphabetical listings of information and videos of seniors' health-related conditions.

www.nihseniorhealth.gov

National Safety Council

Provides information on safety including personal safety in the home.

www.nsc.org

Public Health Agency of Canada: The Safe Living Guide

A guide to home safety for seniors.

http://www2.gov.bc.ca/assets/gov/topic/2038E757D68E49D5DC-8C3CD0061E8E1B/pdf/safe_living_guide.pdf

United Kingdom National Health Services

Provides health information, services, and programs within the United Kingdom.

www.nhs.uk

United States Department of Agriculture: Choose My Plate

Food plans, recipes, videos, tips, and programs for nutrition and exercise suited to seniors and various consumers.

www.choosemyplate.gov

United States Department of Health and Human Services – Administration on Aging

Provides information on aging including home modifications.

www.aoa.gov

World Health Organization

Provides a global perspective on helpful topics, publications, and links regarding seniors issues.

www.who.int

1.1 Specific seniors' websites

The following associations and organizations can provide seniors with information, benefits, resources, and community:

American Association of Retired Persons (AARP)

www.aarp.org

Canadian Association of Retired Persons (CARP)

www.carp.ca

International Council on Active Aging (ICAA)

www.icaa.cc

2. Books

The following books are part of the Elder Care Series, published by Self-Counsel Press:

Caregiver's Guide for Canadians, by Rick Lauber

Protect Your Elderly Parents: Become Your Parents' Guardian or Trustee, by Lynne Butler

Supporting Parents with Alzheimer's: Your Parents Took Care of You, Now How Do You Take Care of Them?, by Tanya Lee Howe

Download Kit

Please enter the URL you see in the box below into your computer web browser to access and download the kit.

www.self-counsel.com/updates/agingsafely/15kit.htm

The download kit offers forms in MS Word and/or PDF format so you can edit as needed. It includes checklist and worksheets to help you plan your big day without a big budget.

OTHER TITLES OF INTEREST FROM SELF-COUNSEL PRESS

Financial Care for Your Aging Parent
Lise Andreana, CPP, CPCA
ISBN 978-1-77040-192-1
6 x 9 • paper • 176 pp.
First Edition
$16.95 USD/$17.95 CAD

Caring for your aging parent can feel overwhelming, from the emotional crisis of sudden illness to the legal crisis of sudden guardianship. A common wish is to be able to provide the same level of love and support to our parents as they so generously offered to us as children. Understanding the potential stress on your finances and savings, and knowing how to cope financially, can help ease this confusing life change. *Financial Care for Your Aging Parent* is a comprehensive guide in easy-to-understand language on how to take care of what matters.

The Author

Lise Andreana is a frequent guest speaker at industry events and holds over 17 years of experience as a financial planner, during which time she has helped over 1,200 clients, ranging from retirees of the 1930s and '40s, Boomers of the '50s and '60s, and young adults of today. Lise is also the author of the Self-Counsel Press title *No More Mac 'n' Cheese: The Real Wold Guide to managing Your Money for Twenty-Somethings*.

Estate Downsizing for Caregivers
Susan Bewsey
ISBN 978-1-77040-191-4
6 x 9 • paper • 136 pp.
First Edition
$13.95 USD/$14.95 CAD

If you've ever been tasked with downsizing someone else's life, then you know just how hard it is to prioritize. It's easy to make mistakes when you think you're acting in someone's best interest, only to find out that you've sentimentalised incorrectly. For caregivers of all stripes, be they spouses, adult children, siblings, nurses, neighbors, friends or caregiving professionals, this book guides the reader through the essential steps to downsize another person's life with ease.

The Author

Susan Bewsey is an entrepreneur who got her start by launching and selling hundreds of home cleaning franchises. After more than a decade of startup success, she parted with her home cleaning venture and is now a development and planning consultant for small businesses. She's the author of *Start & Run a Home Cleaning Business* part the top selling Self-Counsel Press *Start & Run* series.